AMERICAN STREAMLINE

A HANDBOOK OF NEON ADVERTISING DESIGN

PHILIP DI LEMME
INTRODUCTION BY RUDI STERN

VNR VAN NOSTRAND REINHOLD COMPANY

Printed in the United States of America

Published by Van Nostrand Reinhold Company Inc.
135 West 50th Street
New York, New York 10020

Van Nostrand Reinhold Company Limited
Molly Millars Lane
Wokingham, Berkshire RG11 2PY, England

Van Nostrand Reinhold
480 La Trobe Street
Melbourne, Victoria 3000, Australia

Macmillan of Canada
Division of Gage Publishing Limited
164 Commander Boulevard
Agincourt, Ontario M1S 3C7, Canada

16 15 14 13 12 11 10 9 8 7 6 5 4 3 2 1

Library of Congress Cataloging in Publication Data

Di Lemme, Philip.
    American streamline.

    1. Signs and sign-boards—United States.   2. Electric
signs.   3. Neon tubes.   4. Art deco—United States.
I. Title.
HF5841.D492   1984   659.13'6   84-11832
ISBN 0-442-28104-8

INTRODUCTION

RUDI STERN

In the course of research for my book *Let There Be Neon*, I uncovered *Luminous Advertising Sketches* by Philip DiLemme. I was immediately charmed by the quality of the line drawings and more so, I think, by the story they told of the art and craft of American signage and display. If there ever had been a course on integrating luminous tubing in architectural facades, this book would have been required. For a brief period of time the American electric-sign industry looked beyond its most immediate market and collaborated with store designers and architects in creating a style which became known as "streamline." Later it became known as "American Déco." Whatever it was called or will be called in the future, it represents in terms of neon a thrust away from isolated signage toward an area of architectural ornamentation in which signage is but one element in an overall plan. Just as the concurrent and contemporary movie marquee utilized neon as an essential graphic component, store designers made luminous tubing one of their essential building materials.

After what seems in retrospect to have been a quite traditional (although at the time seemingly "progressive") art education, I had never focused on the pleasures of a "Half Moon Inn" (Plate 38). To be used as an upright unit secured to the facade of a building showing two identical sides or as a rooftop structure, this design symbolizes the fluid exuberance of American Deco signage. The DiLemme sketches are, in fact, blueprints for many of the signs and symbols in our American street scene. In their simplicity and directness they are a kind of urban iconography with which we can identify on many levels.

On one hand they are telegraphic images identifying in a coloring-book style the basic services of our urban environment. They are by extension the linear style and facade silhouette of our cities and towns prior to the advent of plasticville. When "downtowns" were composed of these forms and linear shapes they had not only an urban excitement but an electric intimacy as well. They are human-scale design elements no matter how large their individual components might be. Their directness not only implied honesty and integrity but also individuality, no matter how many times they were replicated in a given environment or from city to city. This was not only because the local sign shop intepreted them differently in scale or color or background material but because even rows of them (which of course never occurred) would generate a warmth of design integrity which no amount of plastic surface treatment could approach. They have a handcrafted feel that goes beyond the materials employed. Their richness is in their simplicity and human scale. This lexicon does not offer criteria with rigid rules and limitations but is rather a fanciful handbook for sign shops to show off their craft. It wasn't meant to circumscribe design possibilities but rather to stimulate applications and design solutions using such materials as porcelain enamel, stainless steel, neon, aluminum, glass bricks, and plate glass. Light, both natural and electric, was perceived to be the primary element.

Illumination is now recognized as the life-blood of retail business. Although most merchants know the value of light in their show windows and within the stores, fewer appreciate the value of exterior store illumination as a sales-producing medium. Light, when incorporated in the design of a building as an architectural part of the structure, gives low-cost permanent public interest. A well-designed unified luminous building looks prosperous, and prosperity attracts trade:—*Signs of the Times*, June 1937

Because television advertising has decimated so much of American small business and because these small businesses have so often been absorbed in conglomerates of one kind or another, on-premise advertising has lost much if not all of its individuali-ty and flavor. More often then not those small businesses that have survived employ a kind of signage and exterior presentation that is devoid of personality. In many cases the signage they use is of the packaged variety: generic plastic symbols and letters that neither have visual impact nor provide a graphic statement. Plastic boxes with horizontal grids of fluorescent lamps illuminating their front surfaces or plastic three-dimensional typography with hidden neon strokes have none of the visual excitement of customized and exposed neon. Even a poorly designed neon graphic has more personality than the most elaborate plastic box display. Neonized typography as shown by DiLemme has a kinetic appeal. These signs and symbols were meant to "catch your eye." They were intended as focal points, neighborhood markers, and meeting places.

Television imposed criteria for national taste extolling uniformity and conformity. The products that are pushed are nationally distributed and packaged so as to appeal to the nationwide demographic. The sketches here are for local products, local services, local retail stores. The symbols and packaging offered on television are not open or accessible to local interpretation. Television graphics and packaging are geared to the "universally acceptable" and lately to the "exterritorial." With the exception of boutiques and craft stores, which in themselves represent a protest against homogeneity, local retail stores make every effort to look "national" and not local. The DiLemme sketches are for pretelevision markets where a premium was paid for uniqueness and personalized style. The iconography was meant to be local and specific. The coloring-book quality encouraged the sign company and its customer to fill in color, image, and scale of execution.

Since these designs and other stylistically related to them were still being used in the 1950s, they have become part of our nostalgia in the 80s. With archival thoroughness America has now rediscovered Elvis Presley, plastic dinette sets, Russell Wright, and wrought iron. The dubious "glories" of the 1950s include neon echoes from the 1930s, the true heyday of the medium. An organization called the Society for Commercial Architecture has made efforts to save a few of these storefronts, a handful of such exterior signage and the first of McDonald's architectural delights. In some areas such as South Florida the urban-renewal bulldozers have been restrained and some of these images have been polished up and repaired. Interest in this vernacular architecture is often overly cerebral and runs the risk of being intellectualized to death. The public for the most part has not identified with these efforts to save commercial architecture. I am suspicious of the way in which we seem to treasure the past as we destroy it.

These drawings are electric messages for electric cities. They bespeak our love affair with the industrial age when its negative aspects hadn't yet revealed themselves. They have a utopian, 1930s World's Fair flavor. When I look through them, I can imagine that neon was invented to fulfill the graphic exigencies of their design. Neon was the fluid, electric pen with which these signs and symbols were drawn. Neon was the syntax of an American language in the process of developing. The electric mosaic the

designs composed had a vitality for which this country was known and imitated. The vast spaces and even the smog of our industry demanded a light source powerful enough to cut through it.

A number of the storefront designs in Mr. DiLemme's book are derived from the work of Walter Dorwin Teague and Raymond Loewy, two of America's first industrial designers. They actually carved out a field where none had existed. It was geared to product development and to marketing. Storefronts and signage were natural adjuncts of that effort. Teague's designs were commissioned by the Pittsburgh Plate Glass Company in 1935 and 1936. They relate directly to "Leon's Bar" (Plate K), just as "Melrose Jewelry" (Plate 172) and "Simco" (Plate G) derive from Raymond Loewy's Cushman Bakery storefronts of 1937. Loewy used white sheets of porcelain covered steel and Teague, appropriately, used glass. Almost every "downtown" in America has examples of this "streamlined" look. The plastics that came into widespread use in the 1950s might be seen as a less costly replacement for the glass and steel of the 1930s, although they were promoted as ultramodern aesthetics.

These are blueprints for a more innocent, human-scale American landscape. We are now in a high-tech "cool" period that seeks an anonymous look. These drawings were meant to be flamboyant. They are embellishment and thrive on detailing. They were meant for a slower-moving passerby. There was time then to notice line, message, and image. They were meant to be "down home." They are in the style of an America which has passed.

Book No. 1

A TREATISE ON • ELECTRIC SIGNS

• STORE FRONT DESIGNS

• ABSTRACTS OF MODERN

• ALPHABETS

FOREWORD

LUMINOUS ADVERTISING SKETCHES BOOK ONE AND BOOK TWO IN ONE VOLUME

A short success story about why Book One and Book Two were combined and offered in one complete volume.

Luminous Advertising Sketches Book One, was received and accepted with great acclaim. The creative sketches, art, and lettering were created to be completely practicable and easily adaptable for the various needs of the architect, artist, designer, engineer, as well as the many other people who create, develop, and design practical and pleasing effects of structural and commercial necessities of this day and of the future.

The demand for reprints of the publication Luminous Advertising Sketches Book One has been great, and we the publishers and author together have achieved the full feeling of gratitude towards our many readers. We wish to extend our thanks, at this opportune time, to them for their many kind letters of appreciation and good wishes.

In planning to satisfy the demand for reprints, we had the opportunity to enlarge, revise and modernize Book One. At this time, Book Two was ready to go to press. We decided that the incorporation of these two books into one complete volume would serve a twofold benefit. More material would be available in one volume, and the savings possible in the printing and reproduction could be passed along to our public. We wish to extend our thanks to our public for making Book One so successful.

Author's Footnote

As the author of Luminous Advertising Sketches Book One and Two contained in this volume, I feel that this work definitely exemplifies the electric sign industry and it's applications to this field. I also feel that all arts and designs are compositions of the association of lines to lend beauty and creative feeling to all design regardless of its ultimate use. Therefore, within these pages you will find many lines, designs, and ideas that can be applied in part or in a combination of designs, permitting individual expression and feeling in all fields of endeavor that demand the artistic and creative ability of the individual architect and designer.

THE AUTHOR

Philip De Lemme

NOTES ON THE MAKEUP AND LAYOUT OF THIS COMBINED VOLUME

In order to preserve the full value of the introductions and explanatory material of both books when combined, we have kept the format of the original two separate books. There are sixteen color plates and one hundred and nine black and white plates in Book One. The color plates are keyed by letters and the black and white plates are referred to by number. The color plates and the black and white plates from one to one hundred and nine are indexed at the back of Book One.

For quicker and easier reference, the plates in Book Two have been renumbered to follow consecutively after Book One. Book Two contains plates one hundred ten to two hundred five and are indexed at the back of Book Two.

ELECTRIC SIGN DESIGNING

In the preparation of this book of electrical advertising sketches I have endeavored to present practical material that should be helpful in designing and producing effective displays. With this objective I have drawn upon my many years of experience as a designer and builder of electric signs and spectacular displays. My practical shop experience has taken me through the evolution of electrical advertising from its earliest forms to the modern creations in luminous tubing; and it has afforded me the opportunity of continuous study of electric signs and their function in modern merchandising.

It has been my purpose in preparing these sketches to suggest material that should be helpful to both the beginner and the expert sign draftsman, to give the novice a conception of how to develop his ideas properly in making sketches, and to supply designs that may be adapted as they stand or combined with other ideas.

Sign designing is most interesting and fascinating because every job requires a new and different design. There is a lot of genuine satisfaction in seeing your ideas become actual displays. I mention this because I well remember my first years as a designer during which I was called upon to produce sign designs for some of the largest sign manufacturing plants in the East.

Not many years ago the average electrically illuminated display was considered perfect if the lettering could be read. In general, these signs were ugly in appearance. They consisted of a box with lamps inside or outside and no consideration was given to their artistic

value. Those signs bring to mind the lettering that may still be found on cornices of old buildings. Even the larger displays of earlier years were rampant with continuous scrolls on which lamps were crowded to the limit.

Thanks to the many originators, creators, and designers of electric signs, the sign industry has improved itself many fold through the evolution, and the improvement has extended to all branches of the industry.

As a point of illustration, the sign and automobile industries may be said to be similar in many ways. One could not hope to sell model 1910 automobiles in this day; neither could the best salesman sell model 1910 sign advertising today. By the same token one would not install a late model motor in an old style automobile, nor attempt to install modern neon equipment in out-of-date signs which obviously do not lend themselves to the adaptation of modernistic design or modern color schemes.

Electric sign designing today is a specialized field. It requires a new technique that is recognized and respected by all progressive sign manufacturers. The art of sign designing has advanced to such an extent that architects and builders of modern structures now specify and secure signs of artistic conformity.

Architects who are abreast of the times have discovered that sign designing is a profitable field, and they are specializing in marquee and sign designing. As a rule the designs are very artistic, but sometimes they exhibit lack of experience and knowledge of essential factors in sign construction, and they indicate an unfamili-

arity with the factors existing between effects and the results expected and required in completed signs. The designs may be impracticable from the standpoint of construction and their illuminating effects might be faulty.

A successful sign designer must have a thorough knowledge of electrical advertising construction in order to obtain desired effects in the most practicable and economical manner.

When an architect submits a sign design and plans to a sign manufacturer, it is often necessary for the sign manufacturer's own sign designer to alter the plans to secure proper advertising effects. In doing this it is also essential to retain the artistic qualities of the original design and to make the illuminating effects conform to the original plans.

Owners of new buildings and merchandising-minded store owners are now sign-wise and they demand modern signs that harmonize with their buildings, and their store fronts and interiors. As a result, sign designers are compelled to keep pace with the trends of the times.

Designing Possibilities

Many kinds of signs are employed today, and various materials are used in their construction. In the production of small electric signs, large spectacular illuminated displays, architectural outlining of buildings, and wall decorations, luminous tubing has become exceedingly popular. Combination luminous-tube and incandescent-lamp signs, raised opal glass letters for changeable signs, and changeable silhouette letters for announcing features in theatre marquees, also have popular adaptations.

By simple manipulation the sketches in this book can be adapted in designing and constructing electric signs of all kinds. Careful study of the sketches reveals that they can be rearranged and made to conform with any size or kind of sign required. For example, note Figures 31 and 32. In Figure 32 the design is turned upside down to fit the copy.

Similar twists can be applied to practically every sketch in this book. For instance, the sketch in Figure 8 can be readily changed into an upright design by making slight alterations, such as cutting off the outside square corners. In the sketch shown in Figure 45, the top and bottom ornaments can be spread apart to provide space for either two or three lines of letters. Hundreds of new designs can be created by forming combinations of portions of the sketches shown in this book to obtain interesting variations.

Pictorial electrical advertising displays are growing in popularity, and rightly so, in recognition of the theory that a picture tells a story more effectively than words. In submitting a sketch it is well to consider that an illustration shown outlined with luminous tubing often sells the sign. Luminous tubing can be cleverly adapted in producing pictorial displays in small or large signs.

There are unlimited sources of valuable ideas that can be readily adapted in creating sign designs and decorations. With slight changes, bits of designs observed here and there can be made useful by the designer who is always on the alert for something different and original.

The observant sign designer can get ideas from almost anything he sees around him, such as silverware, packages, buildings, advertisements, cards, furniture, lamp fixtures, and hundreds of other items ever present in the home and visible in daily travels.

The horizontal sign design shown in Figure 19 was originated from an idea given by a paper carton. See Figure 104. Figure 12 shows the development of a design idea inspired by a teaspoon handle. See Figure 105.

Materials For Sign Designing

The materials for sign designing include: (1) a large drawing board; (2) a large T square; (3) a transparent triangle; (4) ruler and scale ruler; (5) pencil compass and pencils; (6) fountain pen (see Figure 106); (7) fountain pen compass (see below); (8) three or four small show-card brushes; (9) brush compass; (10) permanent jet-black fountain pen ink; (11) show-card colors, and metallic water colors in cake form; (12) art gum and ink erasers; (13) heavy black, and white, sketch paper; (14) transparent paper, for transferring parts of designs from one part of the sketch to another; (15) thumb tacks.

A fountain pen filled with a permanent jet-black ink eliminates the use and handling of many drawing instruments. A pencil compass can be easily altered to accommodate a fountain pen. See Figure 107 for details. Time saved by using this method can be utilized to advantage in planning and designing a better sketch and layout for the job at hand. Figure 106 shows the kind of fountain pen to use.

In choosing a fountain pen that will be suitable for sketch work, be sure that the tongue of the pen is higher than the top of the T square that is used. This is important, because a pen with a low tongue will touch the ruling edge of the T square and cause the ink to flow down over the edge of the T square and blot the drawing.

Preparing the Sketch

The usual procedure in attempting to obtain an electrical advertising contract is to submit a sketch of the proposed sign. An individualistic sketch containing the specific copy desired with color and operation suggestions is submitted to the prospect. This sketch should be made to appeal to the sign buyer.

The proper method of preparing a sketch for presentation is to make a scale drawing of the display and dress it to represent a finished picture of the sign. Do not cover the entire sketch with dimensions and elevation plans or make it look like a detailed blueprint drawing. The average prospect can not read a blueprint and such detailed drawings only serve to confuse him. All the notations that are necessary on a sign sketch are the outside dimensions, sizes of the letters, and the color scheme. All other information should be submitted on a separate sheet in the form of detailed drawings for the purpose of having this information clearly specified in the contract.

All sketches must be drawn to scale because they are used for reference in the actual construction of the display. The most popular scales used in sign designing are 1 inch, 1½ inches, and 2 inches to the foot. Do not submit drawings made on very small scales. Make the sketches large enough to bring out all the necessary lines so the prospect can understand them clearly.

It is best to prepare part of the sketch in full color so the prospect will have a conception of how the completed sign will appear. A prospect has more confidence in a company that submits a sketch that is properly prepared and attractively colored. Such a sketch serves as a letter of recommendation to the prospect.

Use a good grade of hard, white sketch paper that will take ink without blotting or blurring and that can be colored with show-card or other water colors without wrinkling. In some instances black cardboard or paper can be used to good advantage to show the burning or glowing night effects of luminous tubing in outdoor signs or window displays.

All black-on-white sketches should first be drawn carefully with a pencil and then inked. In some cases the complete sign design can be drawn on black with white ink. The different colors of the tubing can then be superimposed with show-card colors. A similar shade of color placed around the tubes produces the glowing effect. This can be done with a small air brush or with a small wad of cotton that has been rubbed on soft pastel or dry color.

Perspective in Signs

The following method is the easiest in drawing perspective in making sign sketches:

Use the T square and pivot point as shown in Figure 109. For the best perspective in making marquee sketches, place the sketch paper to the left on the drawing board, and in sketching upright signs place the paper to the right on the board.

In making a sketch of a marquee, show the front and one side in perspective. First draw the front plan of the marquee and from these lines draw the side in perspective from the height measurements whenever possible.

When drawing upright sign sketches, first finish one face completely, as if it were a flat-faced sign; then add the necessary perspective lines to this. The perspective lines are usually made to show the frame of the sign, the height of the channel letters, the height of the border ribs, and whatever other projections there might be above the face of the sign. (See Figures 14 and 16.)

Color Schemes

The following color schemes are very appropriate for modern signs:

1. Light blue borders, bright red or vermilion letters, aluminum background, and stainless steel trimming on raised ribs, or aluminum leaf or paint on ribs of sign.

2. Stainless steel borders, black background, aluminum ornaments, and light blue striping.

3. Light blue borders, black background, red letters.

4. Stainless steel borders or ribs, dark blue background, white or cream-colored letters.

5. Black background, white letters, stainless steel borders or enrichments.

In all these combinations aluminum paint should be used on the frame of the sign instead of the conventional black that has been used for so many years. Aluminum paint is durable and it stands up well in all kinds of weather.

The best system to follow in selecting a color scheme for an attractive display is to maintain a contrast among the border colors, the background, and the letters. The colors used should be kept in complement with one another.

If a light background, such as aluminum, is used, make the borders and letters a darker color. When a dark background is used, make the borders, letters, and ornaments lighter.

In determining the color to be used for luminous-tube reflection, it is a good rule to select colors similar to the colors of the tubes when they are burning. For example, use red or vermilion for plain neon tubes, and light blue for blue tubing.

Gold and yellow are two good background colors for the reflection of such luminous tubes as yellow, orange, red, gold, or any of the warm colors. White or aluminum paint, aluminum leaf, or polished metal, such as stainless steel or polished aluminum, make good reflecting backgrounds for blue, white or green tubing, or any of the cold colors.

White or aluminum paint should be used on the inside of attraction frames such as are used in theatre marquees. This gives a better reflection of the lamps or tubing. Aluminum is preferable.

ARRANGEMENT · LAYOUTS · TUBE BENDING

CHAPTER 2

In arranging the color scheme of the tubing it is preferable to keep the letters in one color and borders and ornamentations in one or two different colors. Four or five colors make the sign look like a color card. Keep the color scheme simple to attain a neat-looking job that will produce effective results.

A channel around a tube or border intensifies the brilliancy of the tubing and increases its visibility. Channels are especially desirable for signs that are kept burning throughout the day.

It is advisable to use red tubing for the most important copy in luminous-tube signs whenever possible. Blue and green are more suitable for ornamentation. The most popular colors in luminous-tube displays are red, blue, and green. Less frequently used colors are gold, orange, yellow, and white.

To obtain good, bright light in changeable-letter frames, I have learned by experience and observation that it is best to use 50-watt lamps placed on 6-inch or 9-inch centers. When luminous tubing is specified it is customary to use three parallel rows of tubing, but the result is a poor and dim lighting effect. Light from luminous tubes does not have sufficient brilliance to penetrate opal-glass letters, such as are usually found in theatre attraction panels. However, luminous tubes in combination with incandescent lamps can be used successfully to obtain changing color effects in such displays by burning the lamps steadily for illumination and flashing the luminous tubes on and off.

The same problem is faced in illuminating the soffit, (ceiling) of the marquee. Luminous tubes are very useful in obtaining decorative effects in this case, but they should be used in combination with incandescent lamps or spotlights to obtain the desired bright, "White Way" effect in front of the theatre. Plenty of light helps to bring in the business and to brighten the spirits of the theatre patrons. The silhouette type of changeable letters now being used by many theatres in marquee attraction displays is by no means new in its conception, but its popularity is returning. This letter is really a substitute for the raised opal-glass letter and most of the builders of marquee signs supply the letters in lots of 300, which is the proper assortment for average-sized marquee attraction signs.

It is essential to have plenty of illumination behind silhouette letters in order to get the proper effect. More light is required than is essential for flat or raised opal-glass letters. The light passing through the opal-glass portions surrounding silhouette letters serves as a background for the letters and therefore plenty of light is needed to get the desired effect.

Luminous Tubing Layouts

After the sign sketch has been approved by the customer and the contract has been signed, the scaled drawing is returned to the sign manufacturer and construction is begun.

A full-sized layout of the sign is first made on heavy brown wrapping paper that can be obtained in rolls about 4 feet wide. The paper is rolled out on a large table and held down with weights or tacks.

With the original sketch serving as a guide a full-sized layout is then drawn to scale with a heavy lead pencil. All border lines, letters, and ornaments should be shown and double lines should be drawn to indicate the tubing. The double lines should be spaced according to the diameter of the tubing to be used, and drawn exactly in the position the tubing is to be placed. A cross mark, surrounded by a circle, is made wherever a housing is to be installed. Two housings are required for every tube unit.

A tube unit is one continuous length of tubing shaped into a letter or letters or design. When the size of the letters is small, two or more letters can be joined in one unit. The housing is a porcelain receptacle especially designed for luminous-tubing installations. When the electrode is placed in the housing the electrical contact is made.

Asbestos Layout Patterns

An asbestos layout is the pattern used by the glass bender to shape the tubes in making luminous-tubing signs. In the process of shaping and bending tubing, the glass is heated until it becomes flexible and it is then laid on the asbestos sheet for shaping. The fireproof properties of the asbestos protect it from damage by the hot glass so the asbestos patterns can be filed away for future use when it is necessary to replace broken tubes.

The following procedure is used in transferring the original full-sized layout of the tubing to the asbestos sheets:

1. Lay out large sheets of carbon paper on the table, with the carbon sides up.

2. Place the asbestos sheet over the carbon paper.

3. Place the full-sized sketch of the sign over the asbestos sheet.

4. Fasten all three sheets together firmly on the table with weights or tacks. Be certain that all the sheets are lying flat and smooth on the table.

5. Trace over the lines on the layout that designate the tubing, using a glass pencil, which is a solid glass rod shaped like a large pencil, or some other hard, smooth-pointed instrument. Then trace the crosses and circles that denote the electrode housings.

When this procedure has been completed you will note that the tubing layout has been imprinted on the asbestos sheet in reverse. The purpose of following a pattern in reverse in tube bending is to make it possible to weld the electrodes to the ends of the tubes, which are finished in an upright position, without having to turn over the partly finished work.

Luminous Tube Bending

In the first operation, the tube bender takes a length of tubing, places a cork in one end, tries it on the pattern and chalk-marks the place where the first bend is located. With a cross-fire or ribbon burner, he then heats the glass at the place where the bend is to be made, giving the glass just enough heat to make it flexible. While bending the tube he blows into the open end with a certain pressure to keep the bend from flattening. While the tube is still hot it is adjusted to fit the pattern on the asbestos. This operation is continued until all the bends in the unit are completed. A piece of tubing, about 6 inches long and of small diameter, is then welded into the unit near one end for the purpose of connecting it to the exhaust pump. This is called tubulation. A tipping torch is used for tubulating the glass and for sealing the electrodes on the ends of the unit.

The next step in processing luminous tubes is known as bombarding. The purpose of this is to remove all impurities and moisture from the inside of the tube and the electrodes.

This is done by creating an intense heat within the tube which is accomplished by connecting the electrodes at each end of the unit with a transformer having a rating of about 15,000 volts, and a control ranging from 100 milliamperes to 800 milliamperes. The amount of amperage required is governed by the type of electrodes used.

The impurities are removed from the inside of the tube by the use of a high-speed vacuum pump, and when the highest possible vacuum is attained, the desired gas is admitted to the tube. The tube is then sealed from the pump and placed on the aging table where remaining impurities are consumed by the electric current. The aging table is equipped with 15,000-volt transformers of 30 milliamperes.

Parts of tubing that connect letters and parts of designs that are not intended to be visible when the tube is burning are blocked out with a non-metallic and non-conductive paint. The tubes are then ready for installation.

SHEET METAL CONSTRUCTION

CHAPTER 3

Sheet-metal construction for luminous-tube signs must be sturdy and rigid. The sign must be so designed and constructed that all faces are rigidly braced and as free as possible from buckles.

Any of the following methods of construction can be employed in obtaining the necessary rigidity in building luminous-tube signs or similar structures. Such reinforcements as partitions, channels, angles, or strap-iron braces are usually found necessary in constructing all luminous-tube signs, due to the weight of the transformers required on the inside of the signs, and to protect the tubing supported on the sign faces. In large signs the proper strength and rigidity can be obtained by the use of an iron frame structure to which the reinforced faces can be secured.

The minimun weight of metal that should be used on sign faces, frames, and backs of signs or letters upon which tubes are to be mounted, should be 24-gauge standard galvanized sheets.

Sheet-metal faces should be secured to structural channel frames by welds, rivets, or bolts spaced at intervals of not more than 8 inches apart. When the sign face is made of 20-gauge or heavier metal, or when the seams are made with three thicknesses of metal engaged by rivets or bolts, the attachments to the structural frame may be spaced as much as 12 inches apart.

When sheet-metal screws are used in place of rivets or bolts in sign construction, they should be so located that the screw points will not cause injury to the insulation of any of the conductors in either the primary or secondary wiring.

Raised or channel letters secured to the face of the sign and to which tubing is attached should be no lighter than 28-gauge metal. If the dimensions of the letters exceed 15 inches, the metal should not be lighter than 26-gauge. Individual letters should be provided with means for attaching them to the background or structural steel frame.

Sheet-metal channel or strap iron used for reinforcing sign faces should not be dependent entirely upon solder joints for security. Such reinforcements must be secured with rivets or bolts so they will not snap off during the construction or erection of the sign.

All portions of structural iron or steel parts should be galvanized or painted for protection against corrosion.

Each sign should be provided with means for attaching it to supports or hanging rig on the building wall. It would be impracticable to attempt to outline methods for the support and hanging of all signs that would be sufficient in all instances. In general, the method used should be such as to provide a reasonable factor of safety in consideration of the weight of the sign, wind pressure, and other strains to which the sign may be subjected in providing service.

The original full-sized layout is used as a pattern or template in shaping the complete sign and for locating the exact position of the tube housings for receiving the electrodes of the tube units.

Transformers and wiring are usually installed in the sign when the frame and one face are assembled. The positions for placing the transformers can be judged best at that time. They should be placed where they will not interfere with the location of the electrode housings, wiring or braces. Convenient doors and hand holes are required in the sides or backs of the signs so that the transformers can be easily serviced or replaced when necessary.

A recommended system for sheet-metal sign designing that has been found to give excellent results is illustrated in Figure 46, in which the general principles of detailed design are shown. A modified detailed design is shown in Figure 10. In Figure 2, self-contained skeleton letters are illustrated. Letters in this type are recommended for use on marquees, roof structures, bulletins, building faces, and other places where box-type signs may be undesirable.

Sheet-metal structures are intended to contain all the accessories, such as housings, transformers, and wiring, in a manner that will keep the interior of the sign as waterproof as possible. It is always necessary to provide adequate drainage holes to insure against the collection of water within the sign.

Sign servicing should be given full consideration. An ample number of hand holes should be provided and arranged so that tube housings, wiring, or transformers may be readily repaired or removed in servicing. Covers for the hand holes should be made as water-tight as possible.

ELECTRIC SIGN PAINTING

CHAPTER 4

The following four methods are the most popular for painting electric signs:

1. The lacquer spraying process.
2. Flat color and varnish. The sign is painted with japan or coach colors and given a protective coat of finishing varnish.
3. Brush enameling. High-grade, quick-drying enamels are used.
4. Brush enameling and stippling. Enamel and semi-gloss paint are used in combination.

The lacquer spray system of painting is generally used in painting signs produced in quantities, and for large signs. It is a very efficient method of painting, provided all the necessary equipment and accessories are available.

The first step is to clean the surfaces to be painted by wiping them thoroughly with a rag soaked with lacquer thinner. All corners and solder joints should be cleaned with a brush and wiped with the thinner to remove all dirt, oil, and soldering acid. All the surfaces should then be carefully dusted.

A priming or filler coat is then sprayed on the sign to provide a base for the lacquer finish. When the priming coat is dry the finishing coats of lacquer are applied. All parts of the sign that are not to receive the color being sprayed must be carefully masked with a masking mixture or masking tape.

One of the most important factors in lacquer painting or spraying is the careful cleaning of the sign surfaces. If this part of the job is not done thoroughly the painting

may be ruined and the job will have to be done again.

The flat color and varnish method is one of the oldest in the industry, but it still is used today to advantage. All galvanized iron surfaces to be painted must first be cleaned and washed with vinegar to remove the oil and dirt. They are then dried thoroughly with a rag and dusted carefully.

A priming coat of white lead is then applied. Do not use too much oil in the prime coat because it would retard the drying and create a gloss finish which would prevent the succeeding coats from adhering properly. The prime coat should always be tinted with some of the color that is to be used as the finishing coat on the background, unless you are preparing a cut-in job, in which case the priming coat should be tinted with the color to be used for the lettering.

In doing a cut-in job, the color for the lettering is laid in as soon as the priming coat is dry. When the lettering color is dry the job is ready for cutting-in with the background color.

When using gold or aluminum leaf, the letters are sized in on the priming coat. The background is then cut in with one or two coats of japan color mixed with a little spar varnish and thinned with turpentine to the right brushing consistency. When this mixture is applied to the sign it should dry with a slight gloss, known as an egg-shell gloss. A better wearing job will be obtained if two coats of the japan color are applied. The first coat must be dry before the second coat is applied. When the second coat

is dry, varnish the entire surface with a good grade of spar varnish.

The cut-in method of lettering gives the entire sign a smoother finish. Varnishing produces a uniform gloss. On signs that require a lot of hand lettering and striping, and where no channel letters or raised borders are used, this method is the least tedious.

Coach colors, which are colors ground in japan, are commonly known as flat colors. When mixed properly they dry with a very slight gloss, but a coat of varnish is necessary to protect them from the weather.

To finish a sign with brushing enamel having a linseed oil base, two coats should be applied. The metal must be cleaned with vinegar the same as for a flat color job, and a tinted white lead priming coat is used. For example, if blue has been chosen for the sign border, mix a little of the blue brushing enamel with the white lead priming coat. The same method should be followed in regard to the letters and the background. When these variously-tinted priming coats are dry, apply the finishing coats of enamel. This method is also followed when the borders, ornaments, and letters are raised, channeled, or ribbed.

The combination brushing enamel and stippling process is a simple method of electric sign painting. Good results can be obtained with very little effort and it can be successfully used on signs having raised or channeled letters or borders.

The galvanized metal is cleaned with vinegar the same as in the flat coat and brushing enamel processes and the priming coats are prepared and applied in the same manner. Only the best grades of enamel should be used. The new four-hour enamels are satisfactory and they set slowly enough to permit time to pick up runs that sometimes develop on large signs.

The second or finishing coat for the background should be a mixture of one-half japan color and one-half enamel, thinned with turpentine to a brushing consistency. This should be a heavier coat than is usually applied to provide for the stipple. The stippling must be done thoroughly and evenly with a house painter's stippling brush. A long-handled fitch or sash tool with a round ferrule is used for stippling in the corners and close places between the letters.

The background mixture should dry with a semi-gloss. Stippled backgrounds make very satisfactory finishes for electric signs because of the processes of manufacturing.

The heat of soldering irons, the punching of holes, and the tightening of bolts all tend to develop waves and buckles in the iron. These defects and screw heads or rivets that project from the face of the sign can be easily camouflaged by the stippling process.

When a large sign is varnished, the high gloss magnifies every buckle, ripple, or slight dent in the sign. It is practically impossible to avoid these defects, but they can be at least partially hidden by the application of a stippled finish.

The brilliancy of the gloss on a sign can be controlled by using more or less enamel with the japan color. If a very flat finish is desired, use one part enamel and three parts japan color and thin with very little turpentine. Stippled aluminum backgrounds with red letters and light blue borders provide a popular color scheme for use on modern electric signs.

Changeable letters for attraction panels on marquees may be hand painted, sprayed, or dipped with brushing lacquer or enamel. A special factory-mixed dipping paint is required for the dipping method of painting letters. Ordinary lacquer and quick-drying enamels set too rapidly, causing runs in the paint to set. Black or a color to match the marquee background is customarily used for this purpose. Before painting the letters they must be cleaned thoroughly with the lacquer thinner recommended for the brand of lacquer being used. A handy drying rack for stacking changeable letters that have been painted is illustrated in Figure 108.

The painting directions I have given are based on the presumption that only the best quality paints are used. It is the quality and not the quantity of paint applied to a sign that produces the best results.

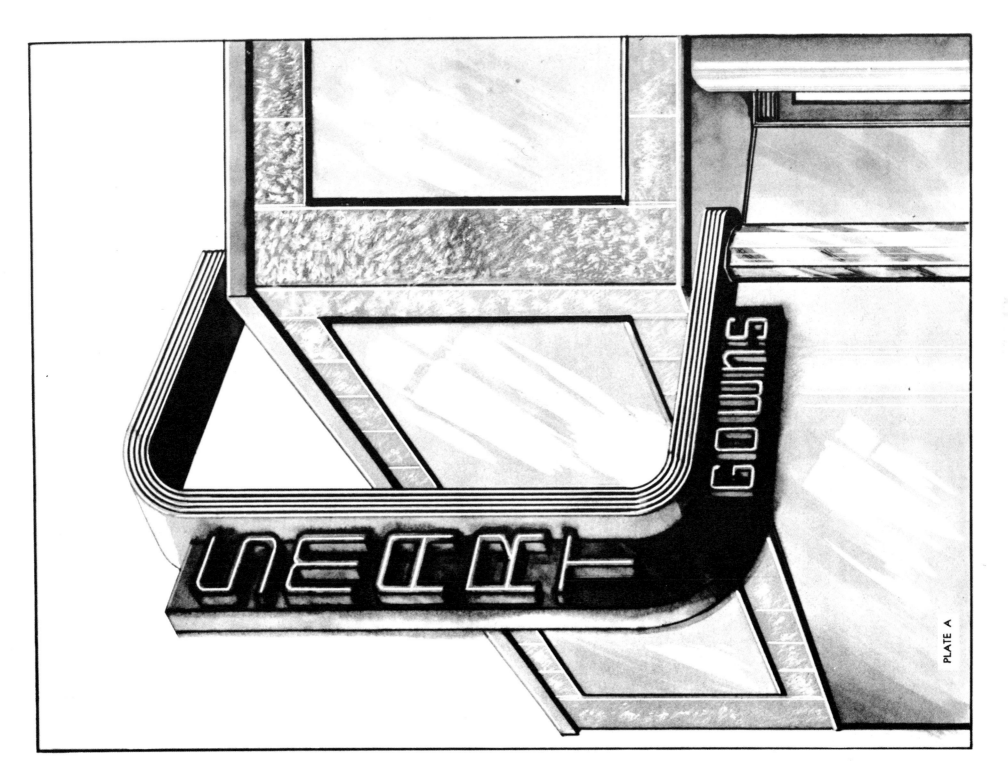

PLATE A

PLATE B

PLATE C

PLATE D

PLATE E

Stella Hosiery

107

PLATE F

PLATE G

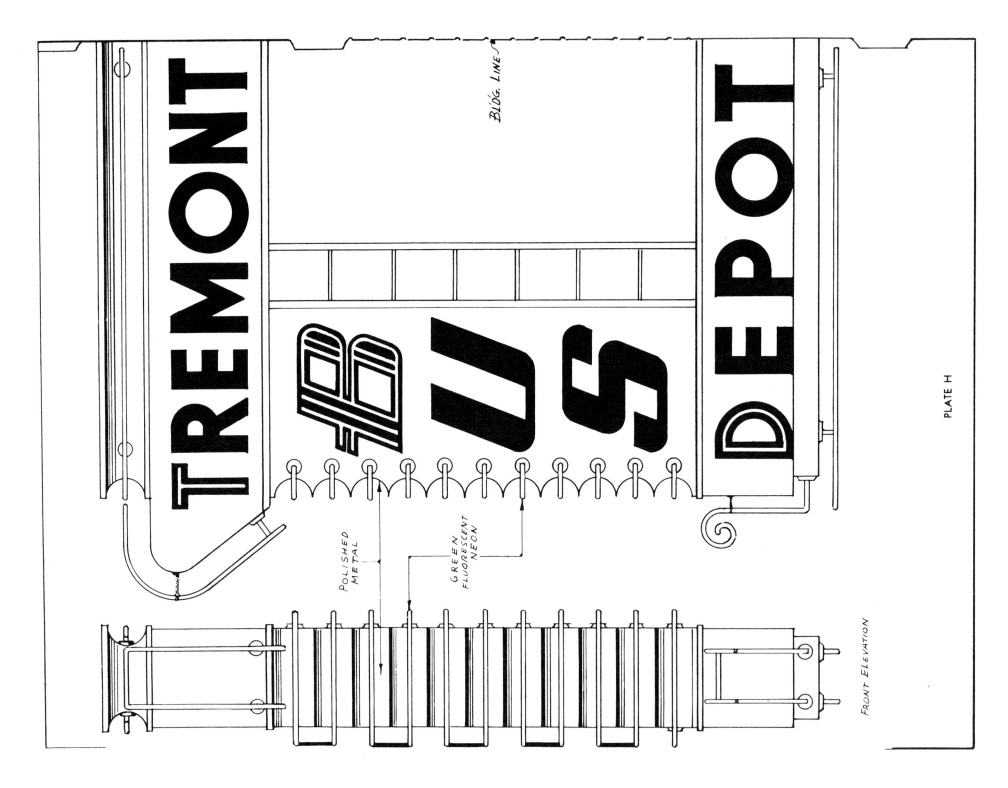

TREMONT

BUS

DEPOT

BLDG. LINE

POLISHED METAL

GREEN FLUORESCENT NEON

FRONT ELEVATION

PLATE H

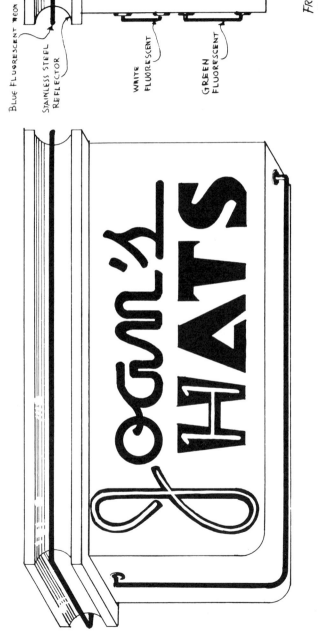

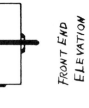

BLUE FLUORESCENT NEON

STAINLESS STEEL REFLECTOR

WHITE FLUORESCENT

GREEN FLUORESCENT

FRONT END ELEVATION

LOGAN'S HATS

PLATE I

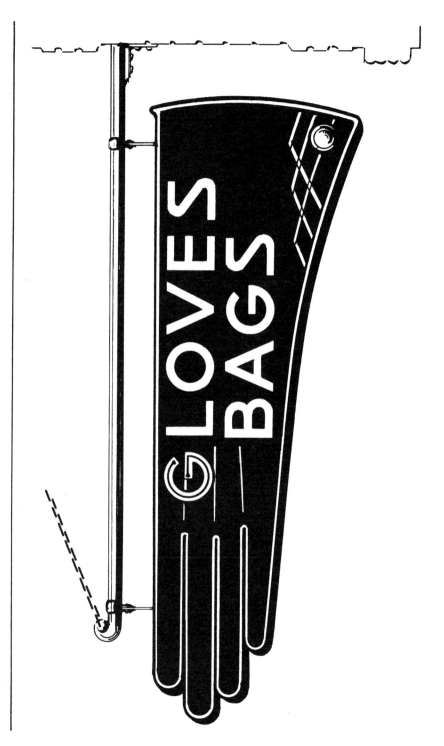

GLOVES BAGS

PLATE J

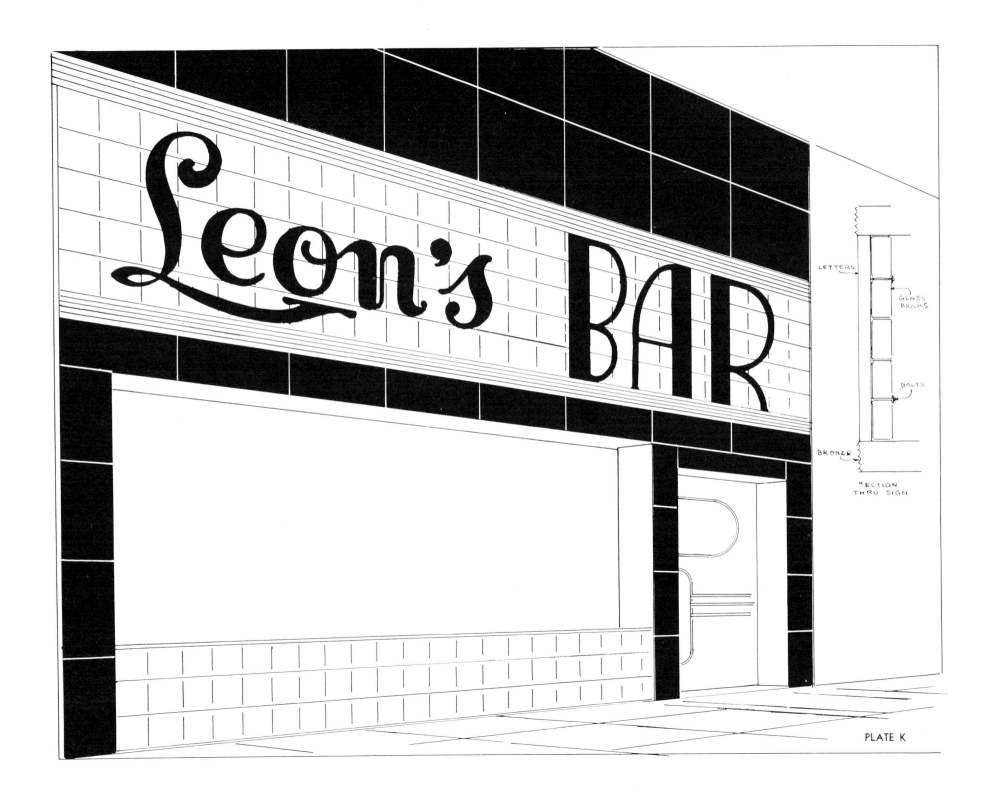

LETTERS

GLASS BRICKS

BOLTS

BRONZE

SECTION
THRU SIGN

PLATE K

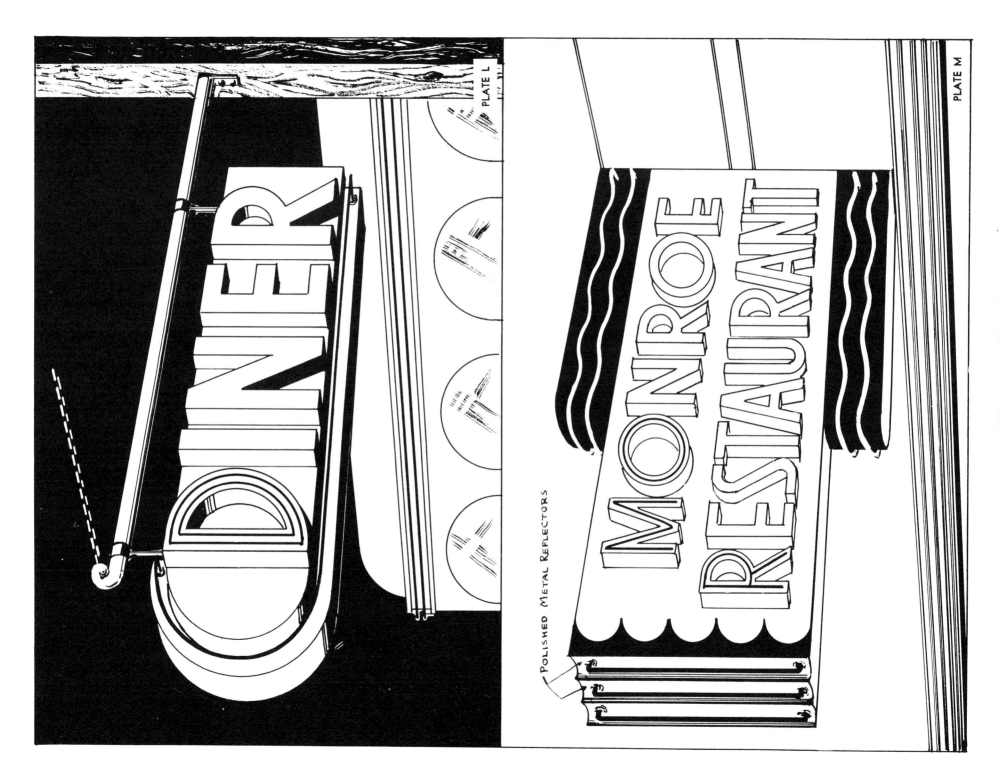

PLATE L

DINER

MONROE RESTAURANT

POLISHED METAL REFLECTORS

ALBERT'S PERMANENTS

DAVID'S
HAIR STYLISTS

LETTERS 8" DEEP

PLATE O

STRIP LIGHT
LAMPS 6" O.C.

SECTION THRU
SIGN

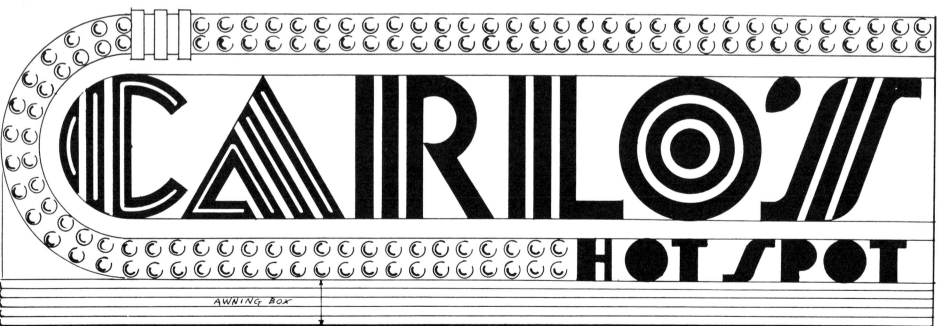

CARLO'S
HOT SPOT

AWNING BOX

PLATE P

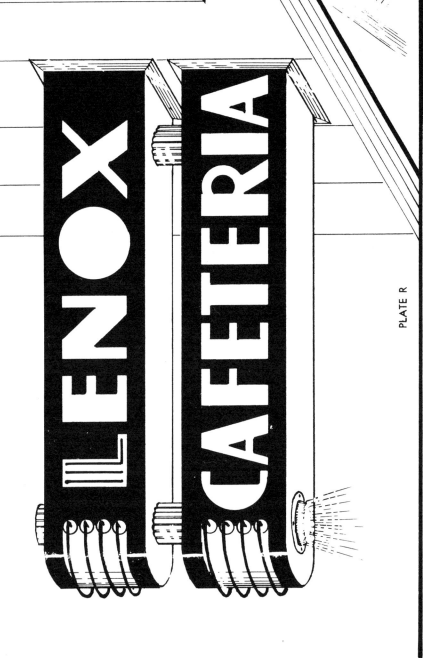

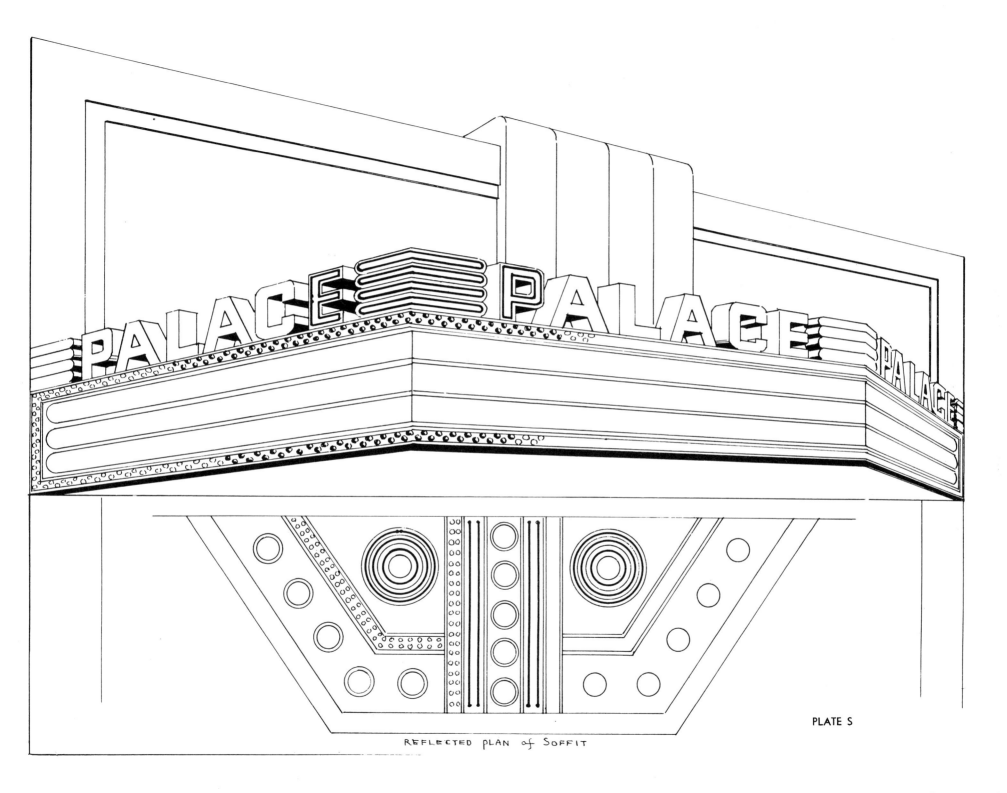

REFLECTED PLAN of SOFFIT

PLATE S

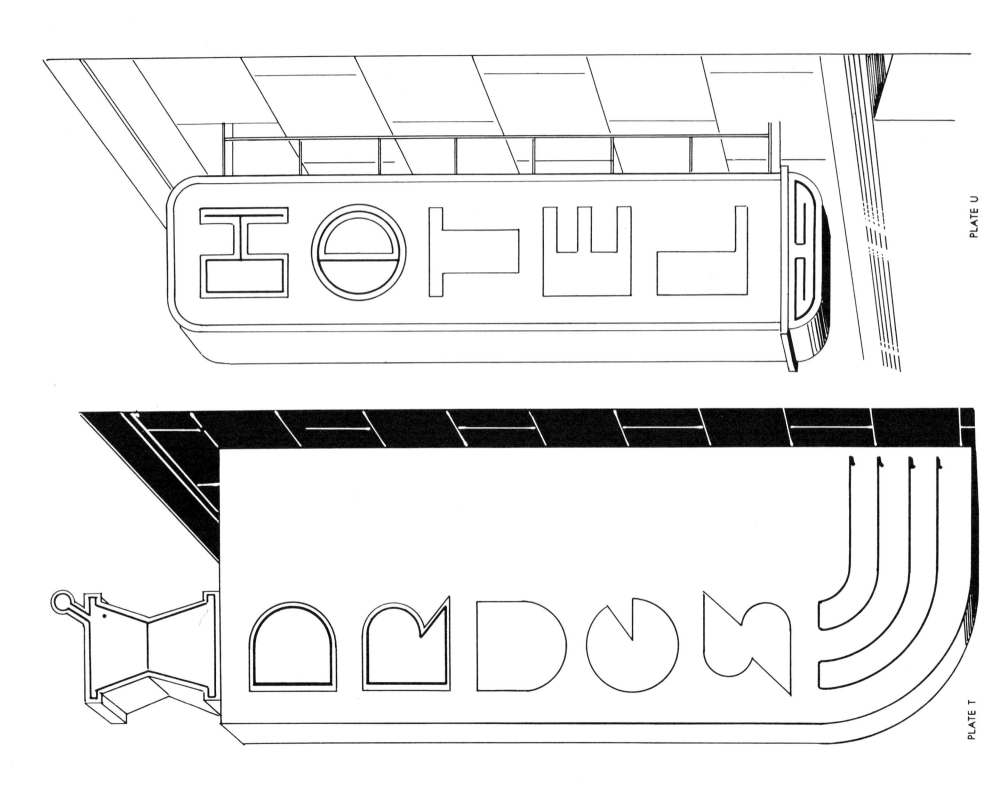

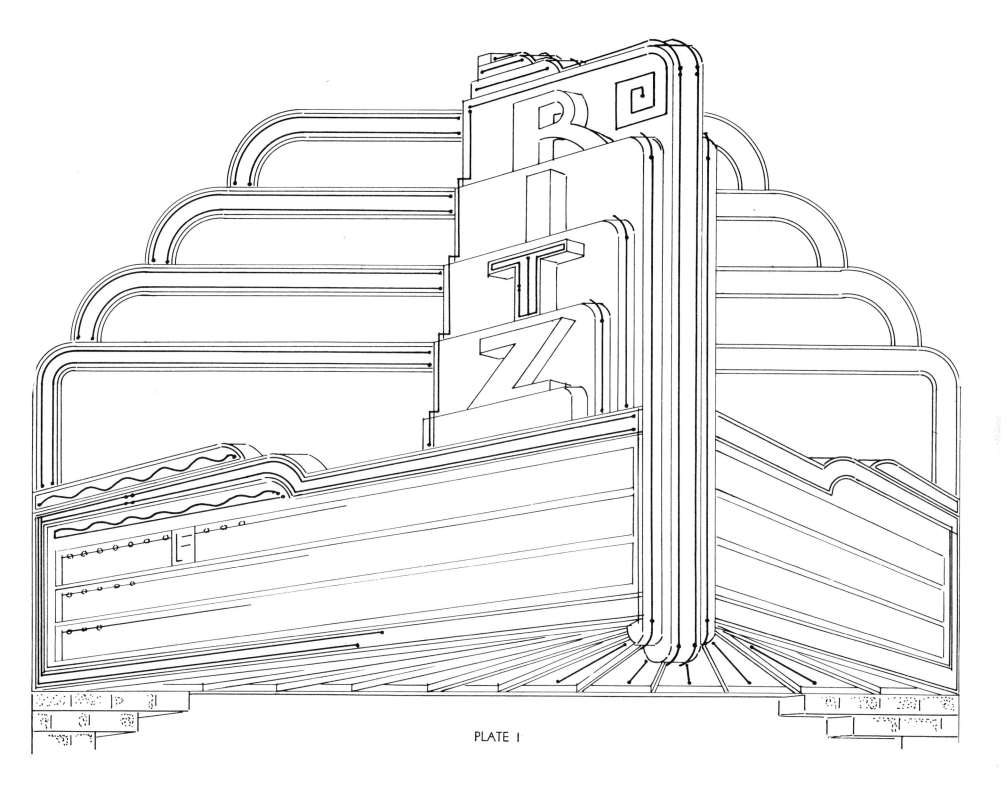

PLATE I

A·B·C·D — SPOTLIGHTS

PLATE 2

NOVO

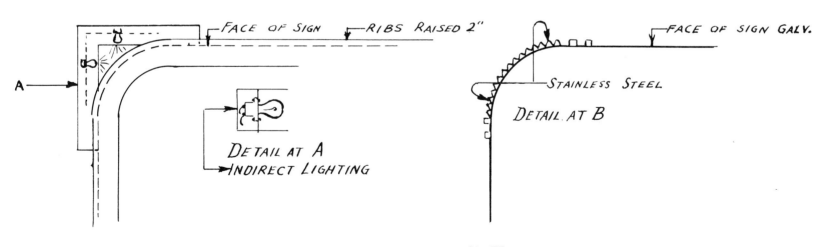

FACE OF SIGN — RIBS RAISED 2"

FACE OF SIGN GALV.

STAINLESS STEEL

DETAIL AT B

DETAIL AT A
INDIRECT LIGHTING

PLATE 3

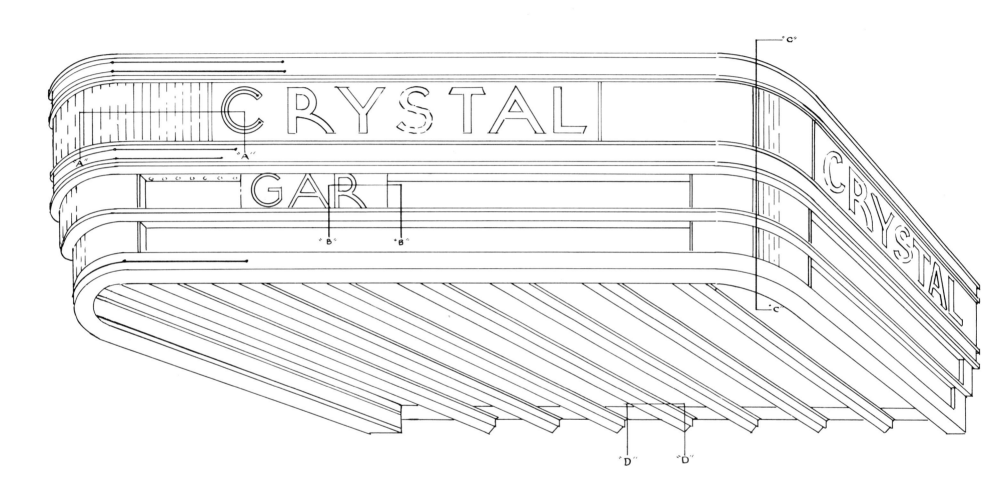

PLATE 4

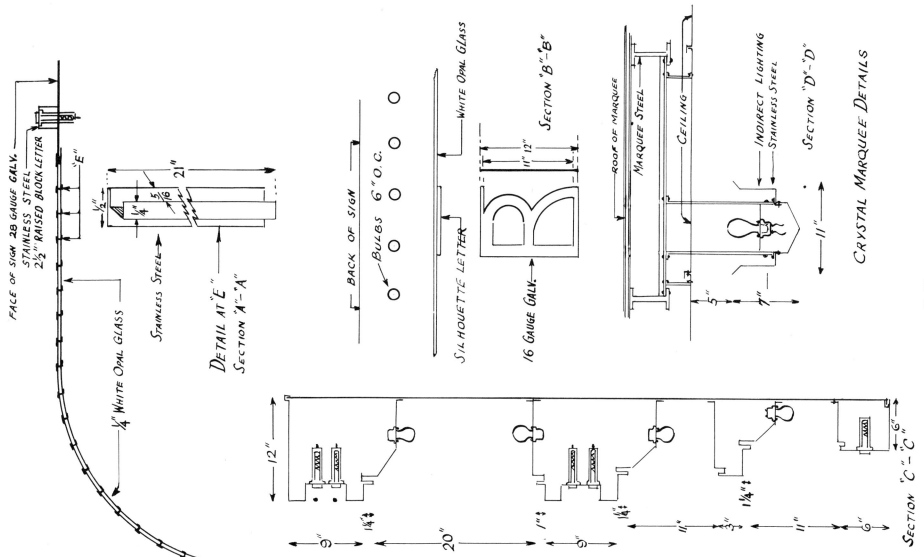

FACE OF SIGN 28 GAUGE GALV.
STAINLESS STEEL
2½" RAISED BLOCK LETTER

"E"

21"

½"
¼" 5/16

STAINLESS STEEL

DETAIL AT "E"
SECTION "A"–"A"

¼" WHITE OPAL GLASS

BACK OF SIGN

BULBS 6" O.C.

WHITE OPAL GLASS

SILHOUETTE LETTER

12"
11"

SECTION "B"–"B"

16 GAUGE GALV.

ROOF OF MARQUEE

MARQUEE STEEL

CEILING

INDIRECT LIGHTING
STAINLESS STEEL

11"

5"   7"

SECTION "D"–"D"

CRYSTAL MARQUEE DETAILS

12"

9"   20"   9"   11"   3"   11"   6"

1¼"‡   1"‡   1¼"‡

6"

SECTION "C"–"C"

PLATE 5

PLATE 6

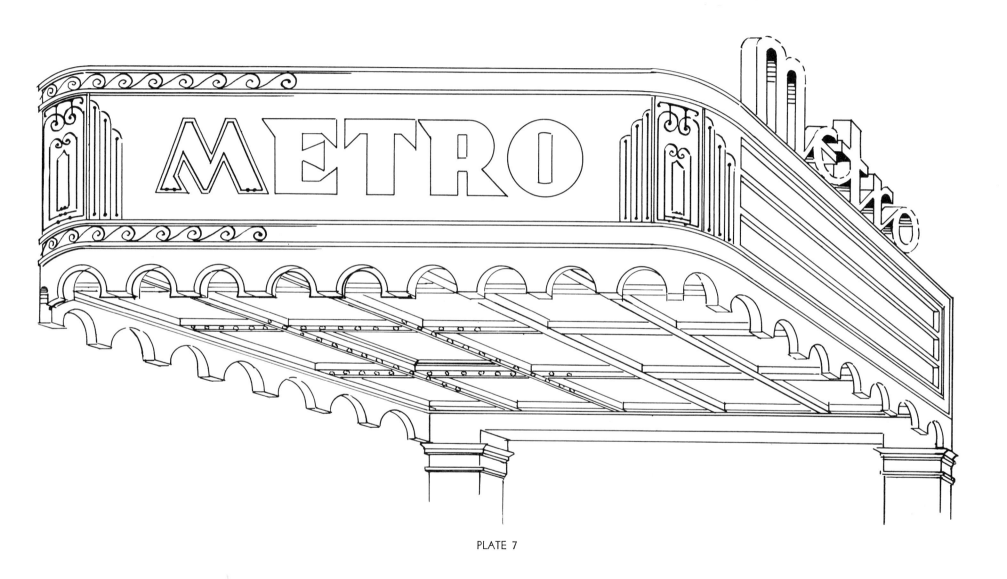

PLATE 7

PLATE 8

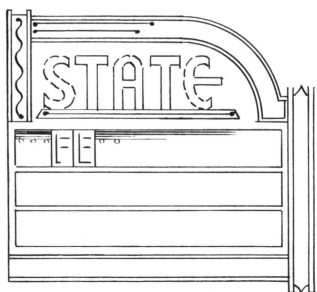

PLATE 9

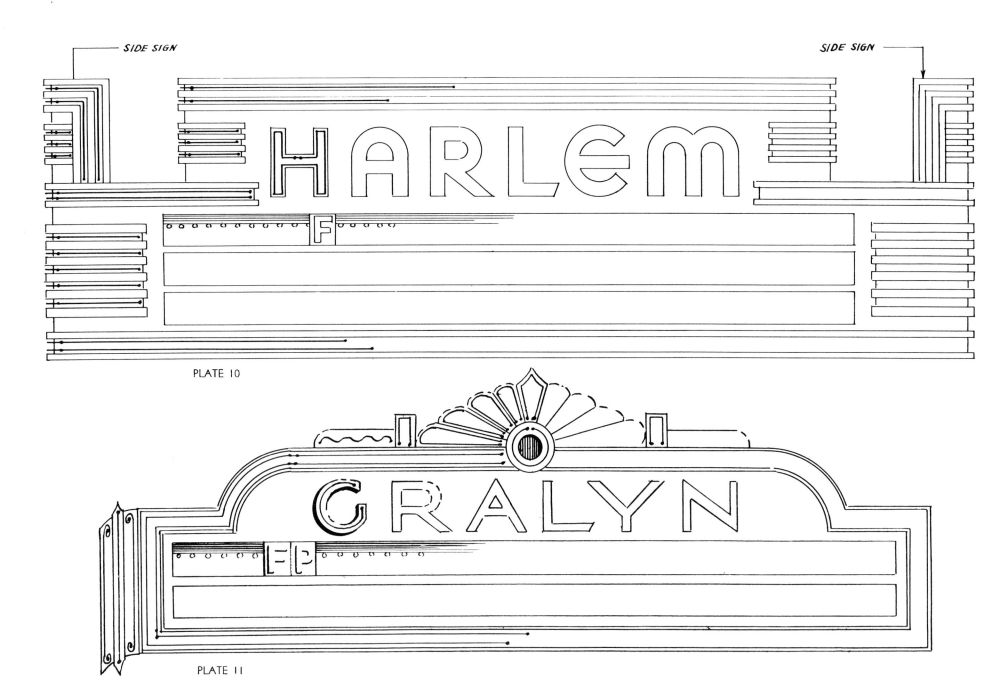

SIDE SIGN

SIDE SIGN

HARLEM

PLATE 10

GRALYN

PLATE 11

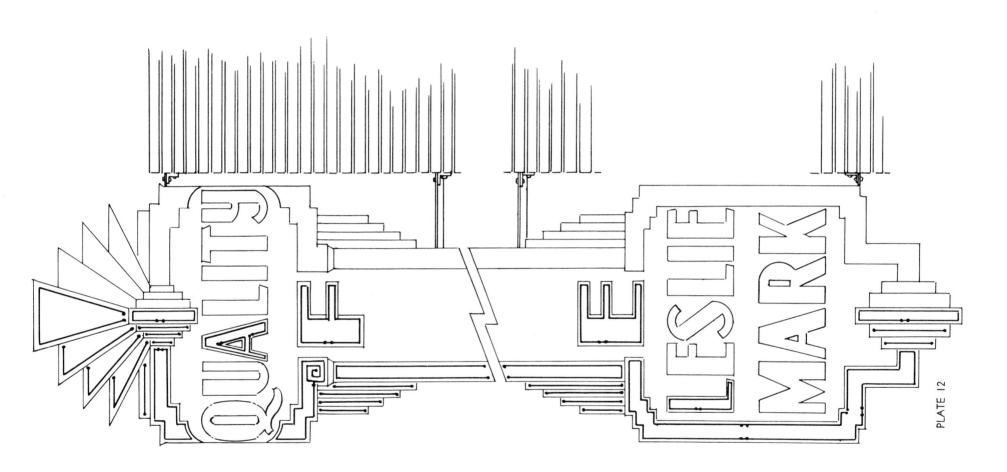

PLATE 12

PLATE 14

PLATE 13

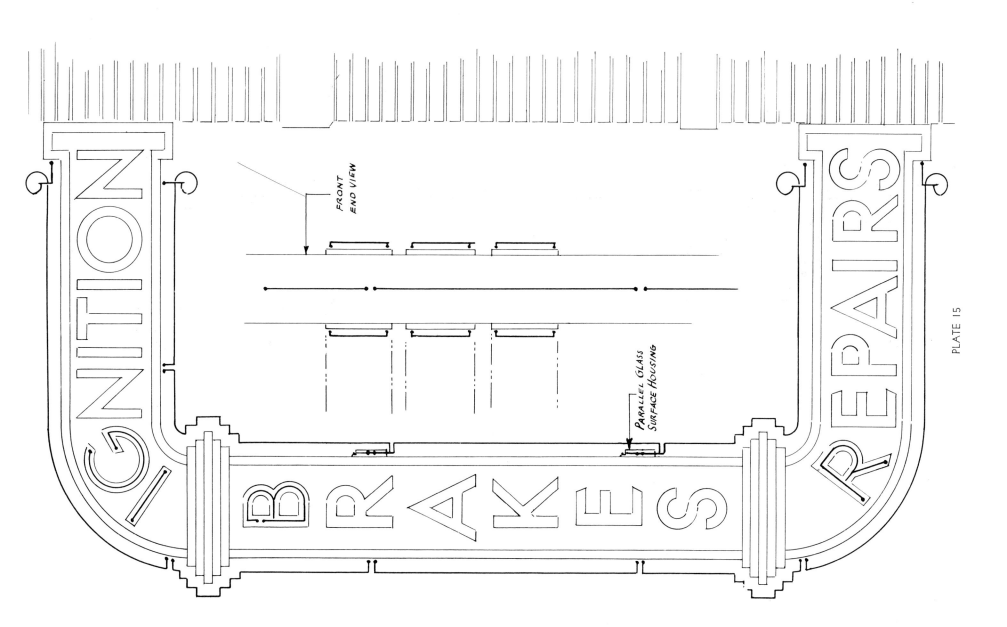

FRONT END VIEW

PARALLEL GLASS
SURFACE HOUSING

IGNITION BRAKES REPAIRS

PLATE 15

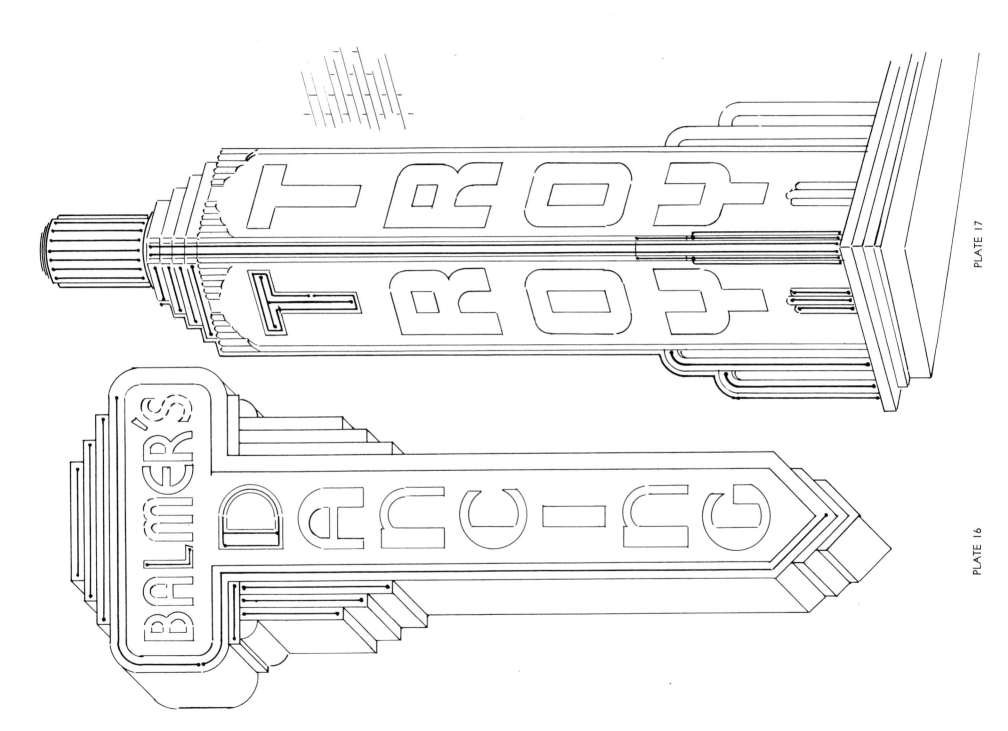

PLATE 17

PLATE 16

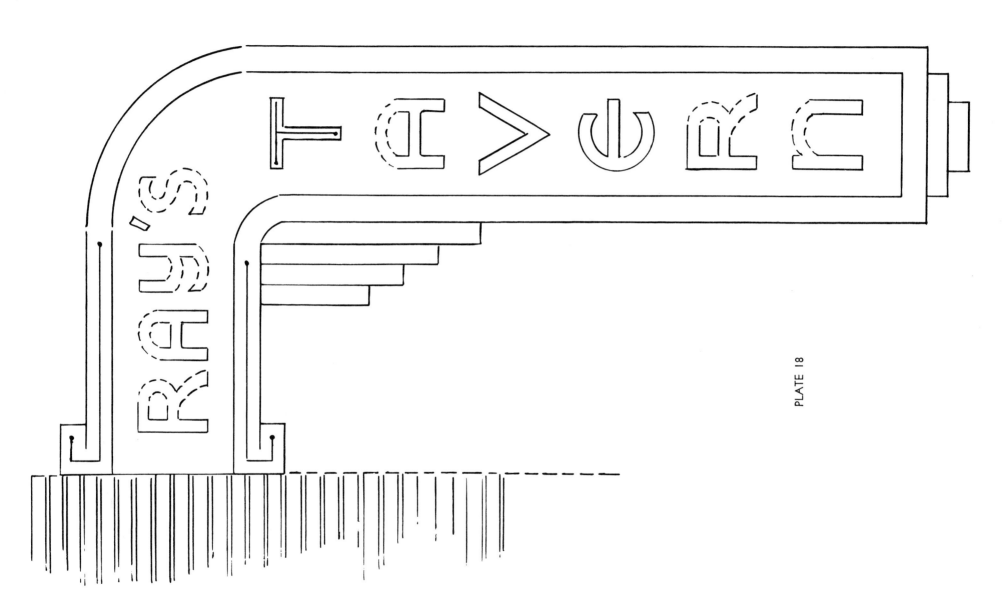

PLATE 18

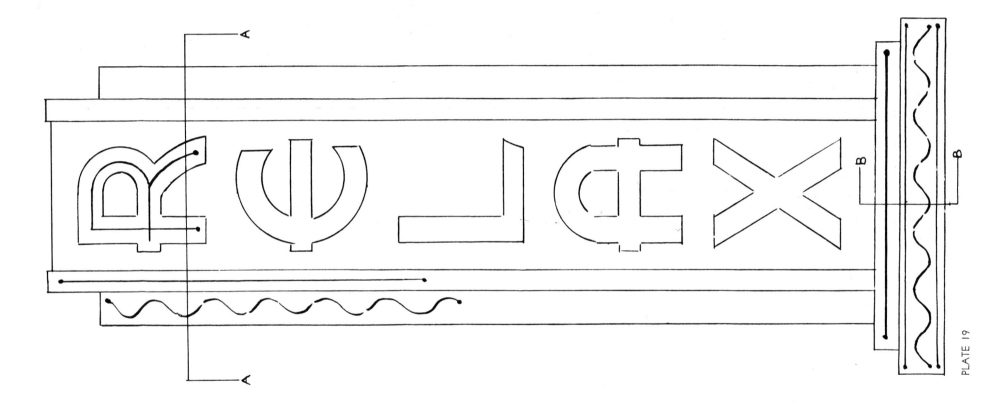

PLATE 19

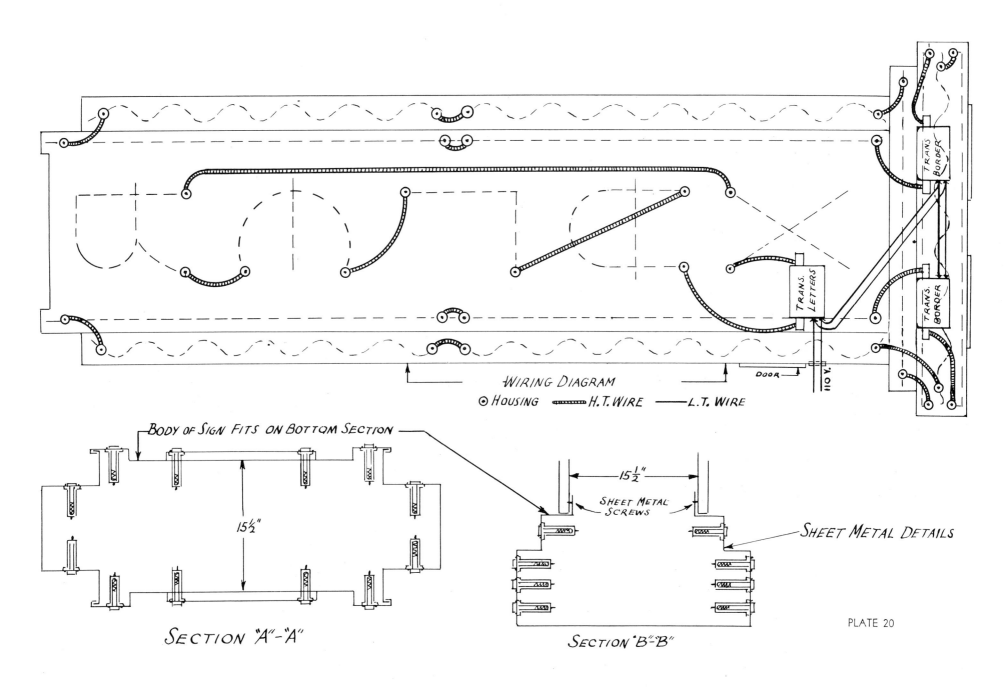

WIRING DIAGRAM

⊙ HOUSING ░░░░ H.T. WIRE ━━ L.T. WIRE

TRANS.
BORDER

TRANS.
BORDER

TRANS.
LETTERS

DOOR

110 V.

BODY OF SIGN FITS ON BOTTOM SECTION

$15\frac{1}{2}''$

SECTION "A"-"A"

$15\frac{1}{2}''$

SHEET METAL
SCREWS

SHEET METAL DETAILS

SECTION "B"-"B"

PLATE 20

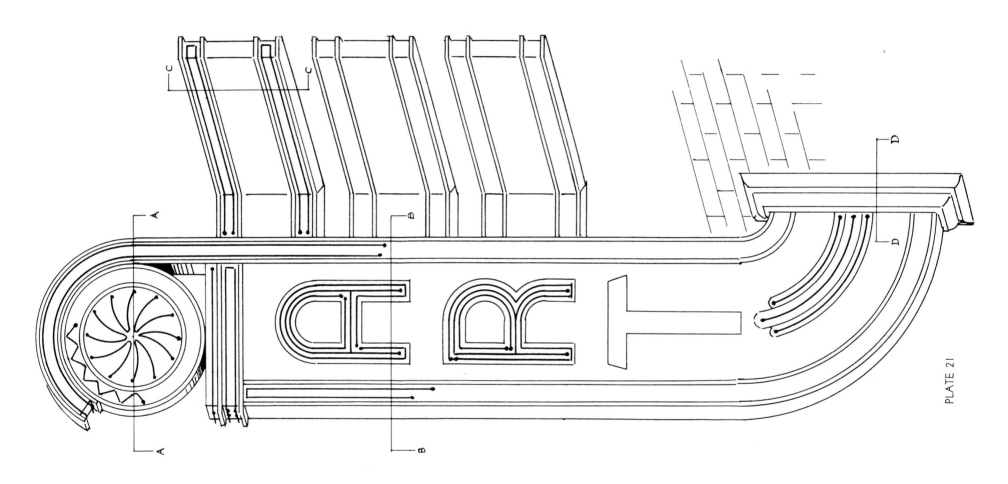

PLATE 21

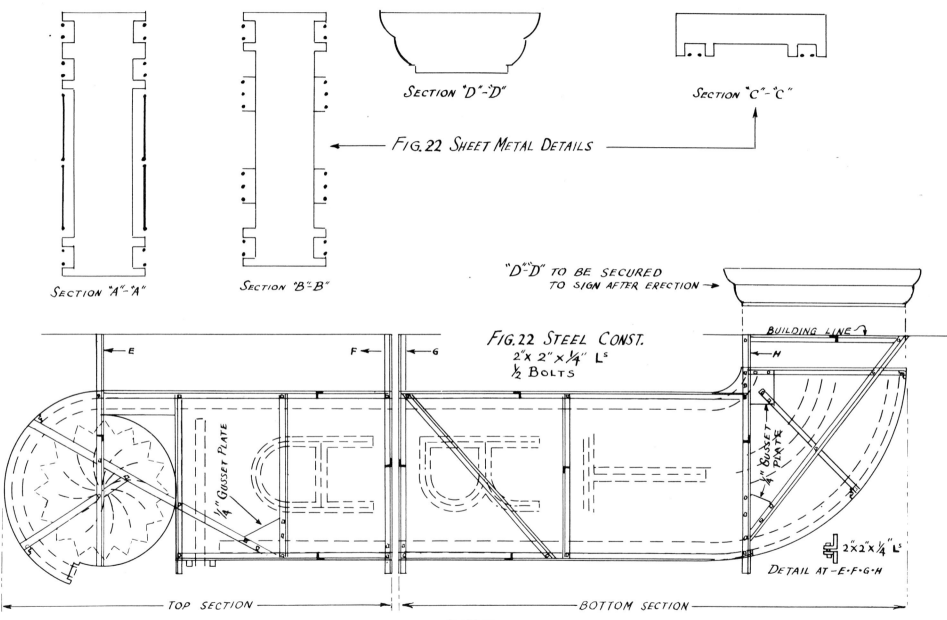

SECTION "D"-"D"

SECTION "C"-"C"

SECTION "A"-"A"

SECTION "B"-"B"

FIG. 22 SHEET METAL DETAILS

"D"-"D" TO BE SECURED
TO SIGN AFTER ERECTION

BUILDING LINE

FIG. 22 STEEL CONST.
2" x 2" x ¼" L^s
½ BOLTS

E   F   G   H

¼" GUSSET PLATE

¼" GUSSET PLATE

2" x 2" x ¼" L^s
DETAIL AT - E·F·G·H

TOP SECTION

BOTTOM SECTION

PLATE 22

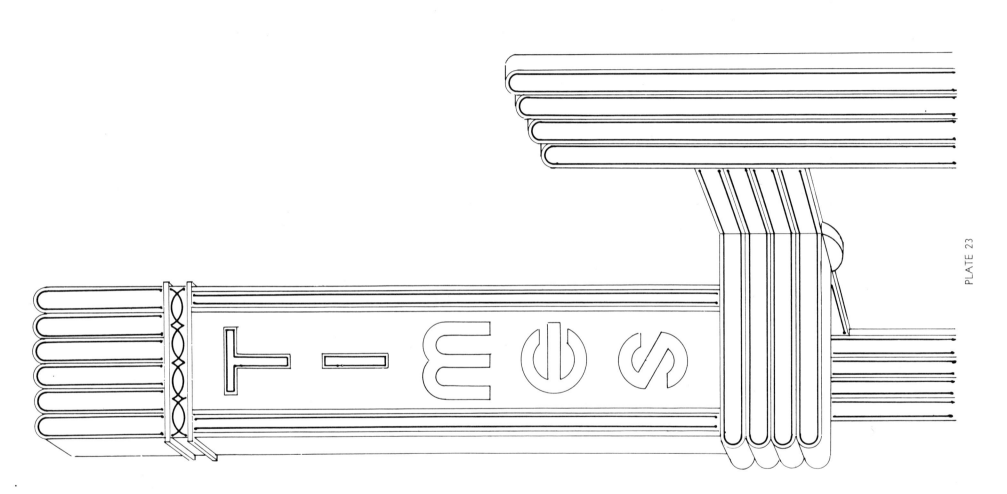

PLATE 23

PLATE 24

PLATE 26

PLATE 25

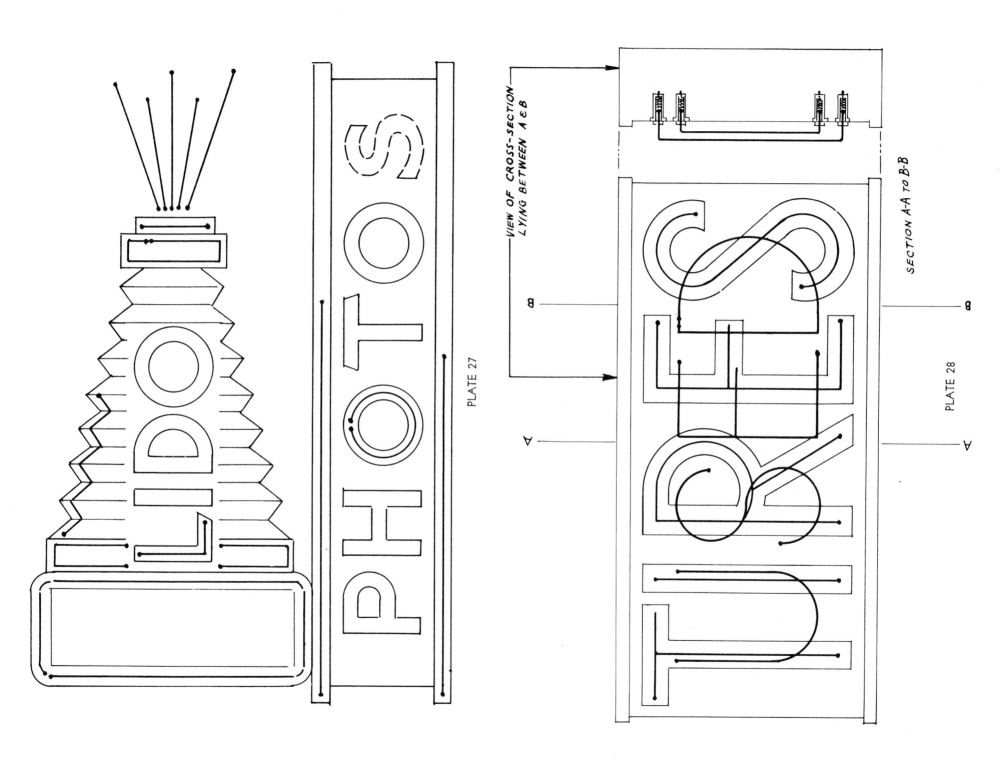

PLATE 27

PLATE 28

VIEW OF CROSS-SECTION LYING BETWEEN A & B

SECTION A-A TO B-B

PLATE 29

PLATE 30

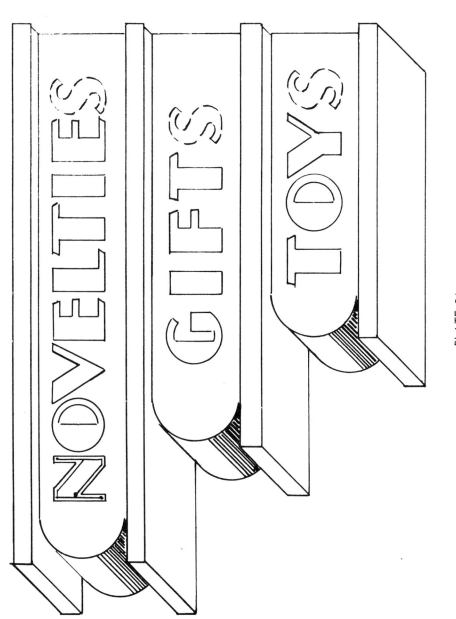

PLATE 31

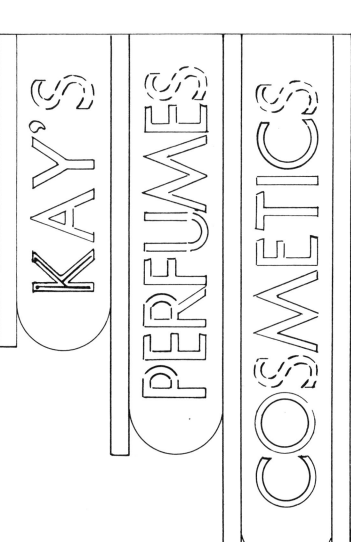

PLATE 32

PLATE 33

PLATE 34

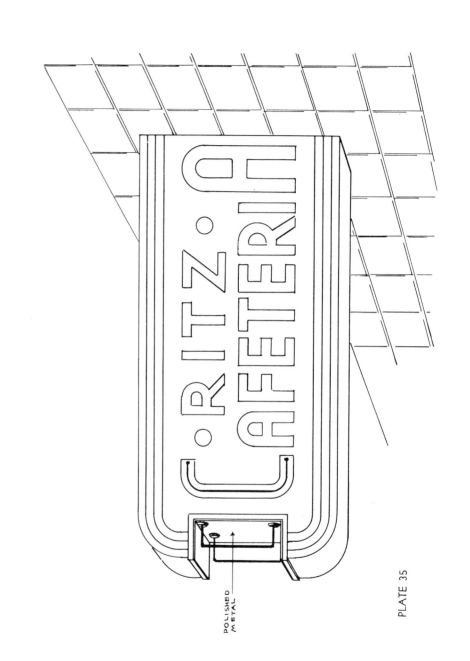

POLISHED
METAL

PLATE 35

PLATE 36

PLATE 37

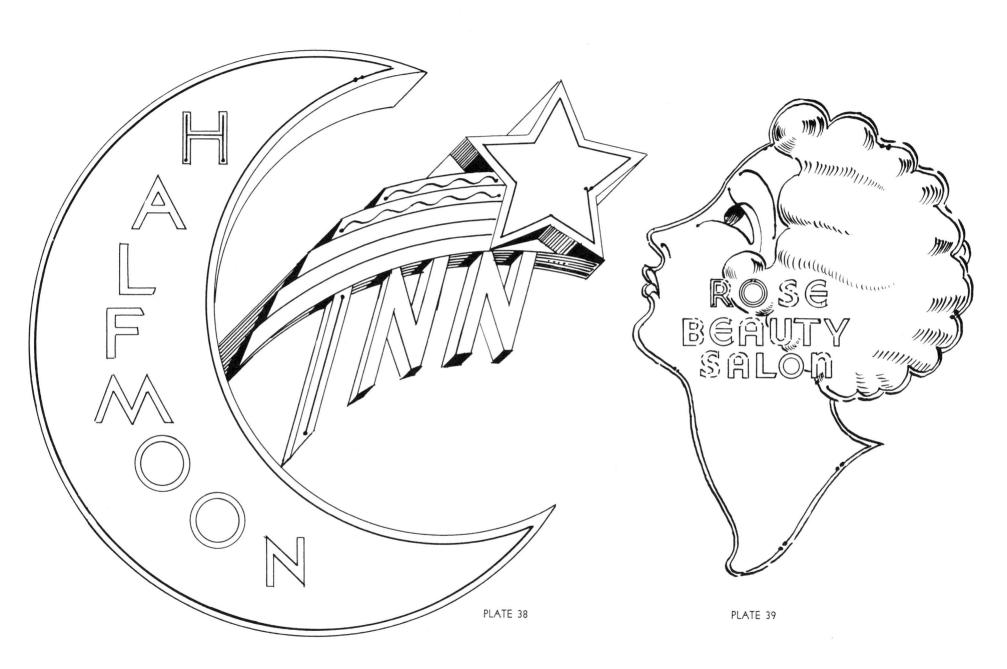

HALF MOON INN

ROSE BEAUTY SALON

PLATE 38

PLATE 39

YORK MARKET INC.

PLATE 41

LIVE POULTRY

PLATE 40

FRYLER'S

PLATE 42

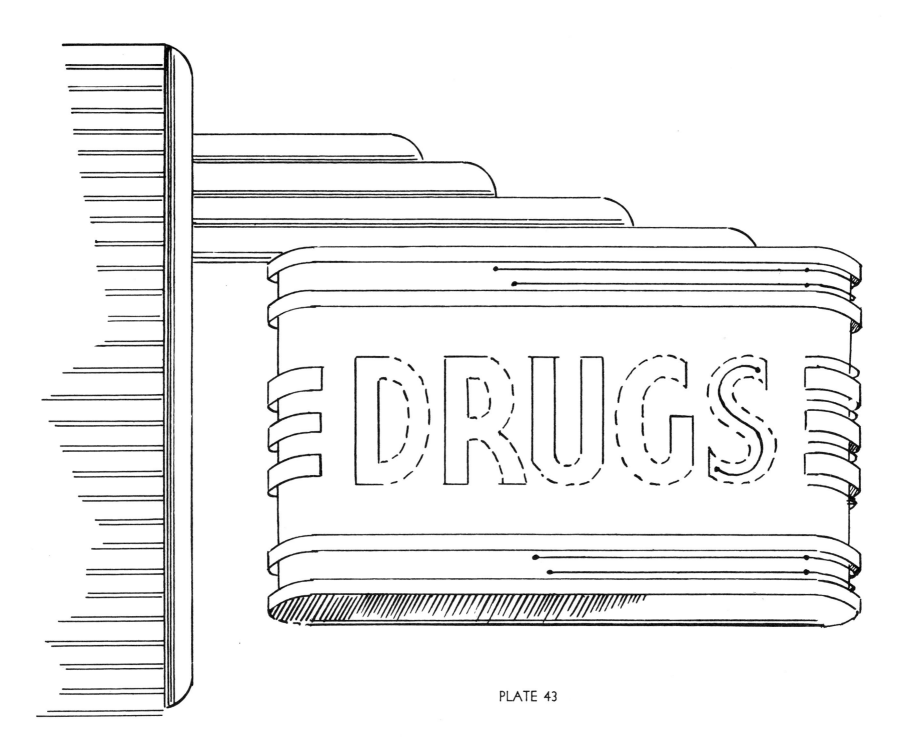

PLATE 43

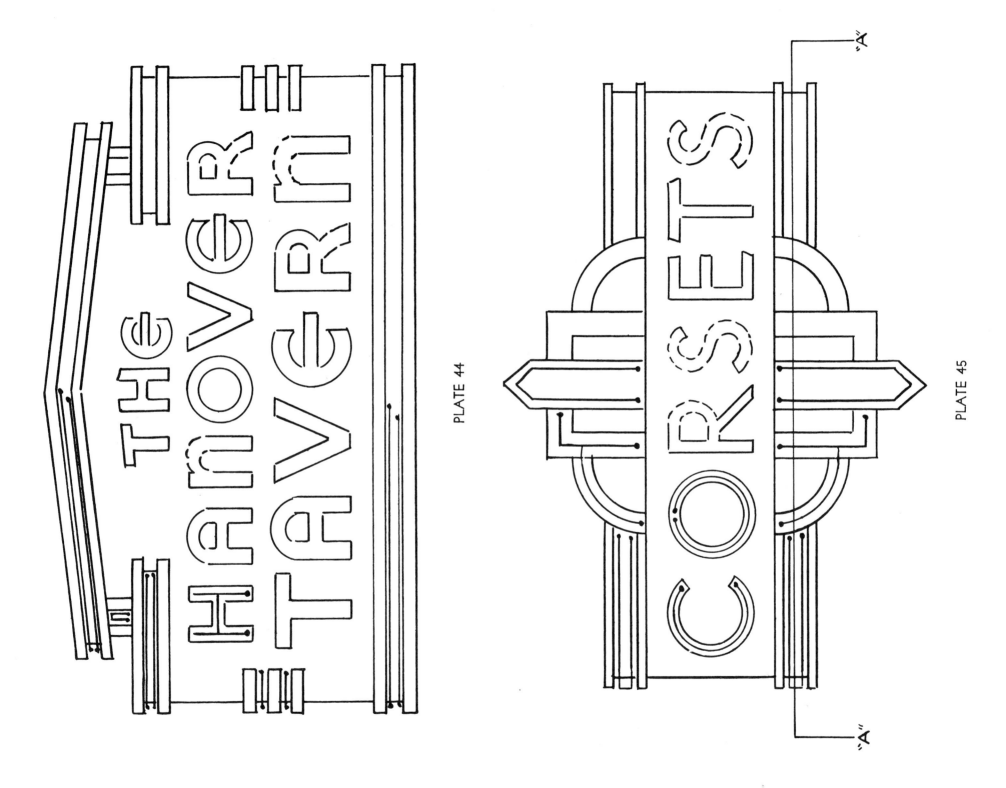

PLATE 44

PLATE 45

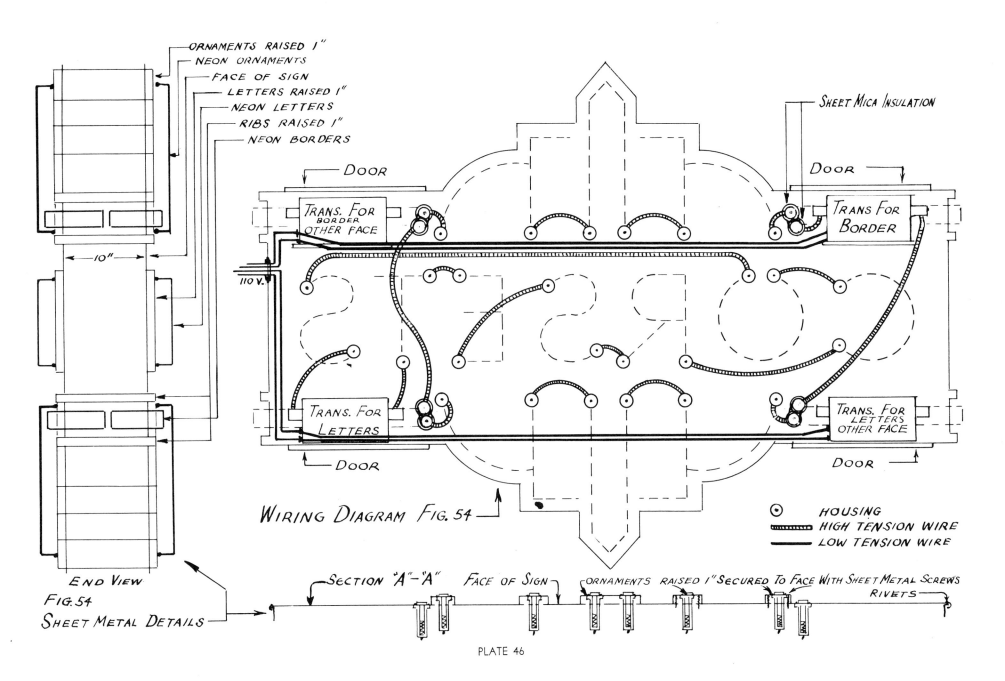

ORNAMENTS RAISED 1"
NEON ORNAMENTS
FACE OF SIGN
LETTERS RAISED 1"
NEON LETTERS
RIBS RAISED 1"
NEON BORDERS

SHEET MICA INSULATION

DOOR

DOOR

TRANS. FOR BORDER OTHER FACE

TRANS FOR BORDER

110 V.

TRANS. FOR LETTERS

TRANS. FOR LETTERS OTHER FACE

DOOR

DOOR

10"

WIRING DIAGRAM FIG. 54

⊙ HOUSING
▥ HIGH TENSION WIRE
━ LOW TENSION WIRE

END VIEW
FIG. 54
SHEET METAL DETAILS

SECTION "A"-"A"   FACE OF SIGN   ORNAMENTS RAISED 1" SECURED TO FACE WITH SHEET METAL SCREWS
RIVETS

PLATE 46

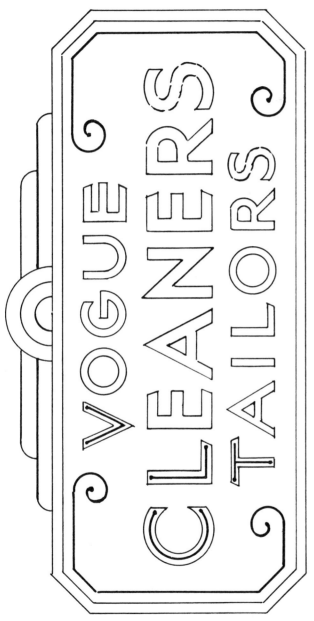

VOGUE CLEANERS TAILORS

PLATE 47

R & M · BAKERY & LUNCH

PLATE 48

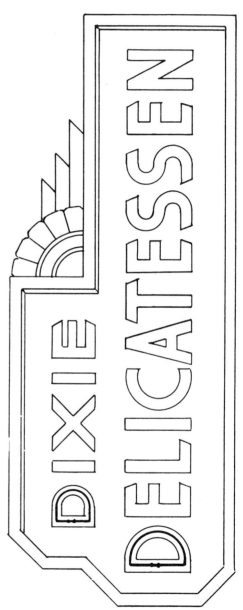

DIXIE DELICATESSEN

PLATE 49

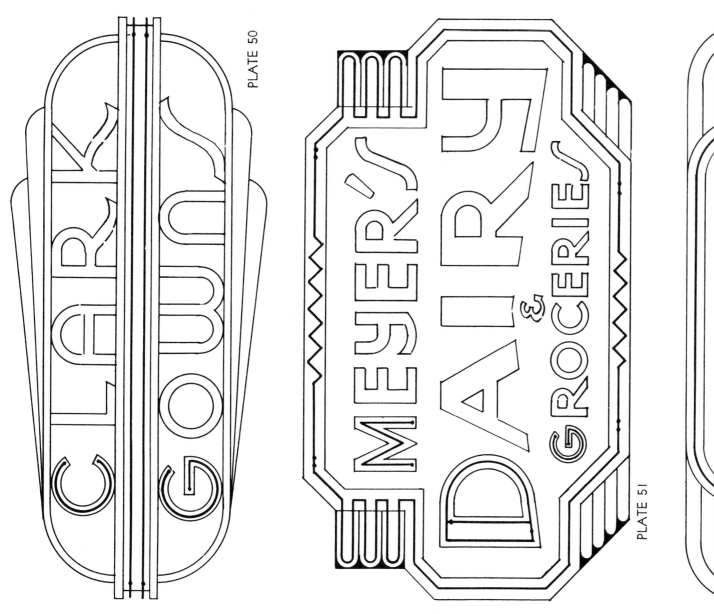

CLARK GOWNS

PLATE 50

MEYER'S DAIRY & GROCERIES

PLATE 51

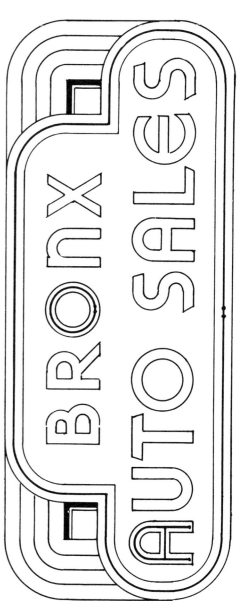

BRONX AUTO SALES

PLATE 52

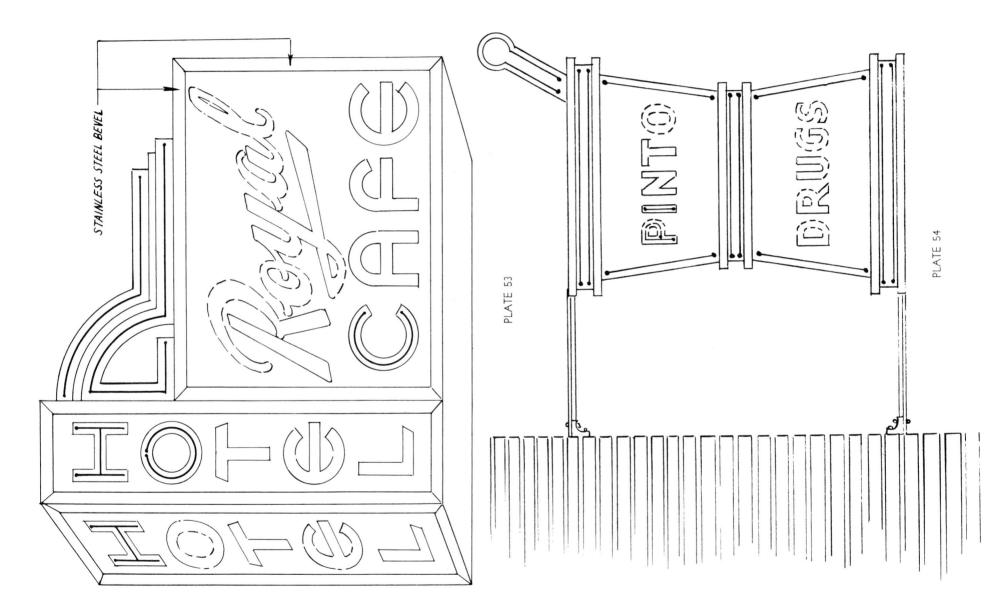

STAINLESS STEEL BEVEL

PLATE 53

PLATE 54

PLATE 55

PLATE 56

PLATE 57

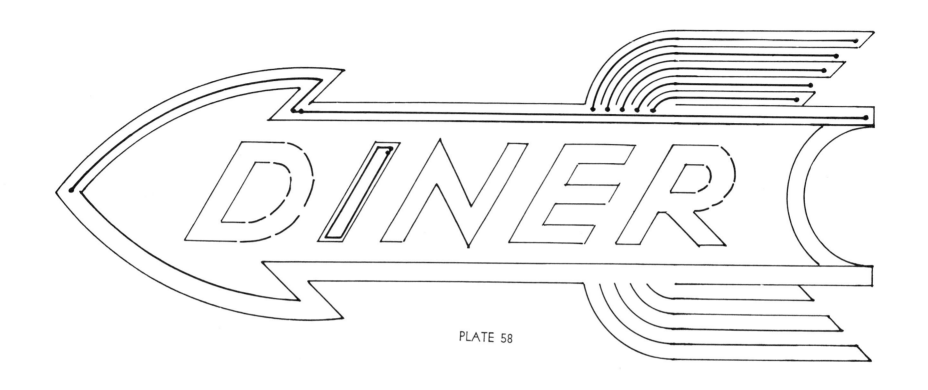

PLATE 58

PLATE 59

PLATE 60

PLATE 61

PLATE 62

PLATE 63

TOP VIEW

PLATE 64

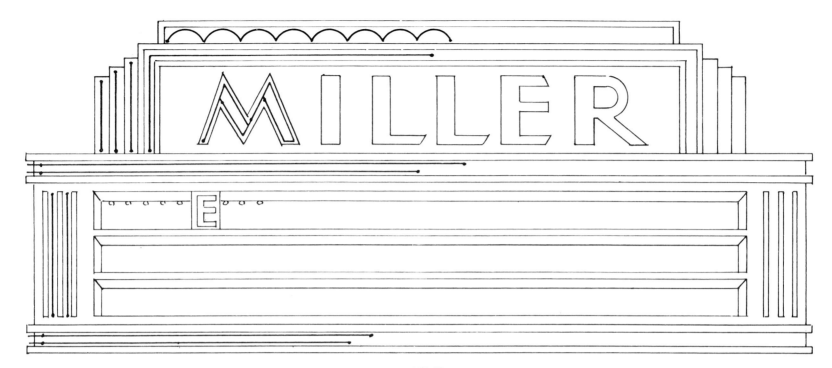

PLATE 65

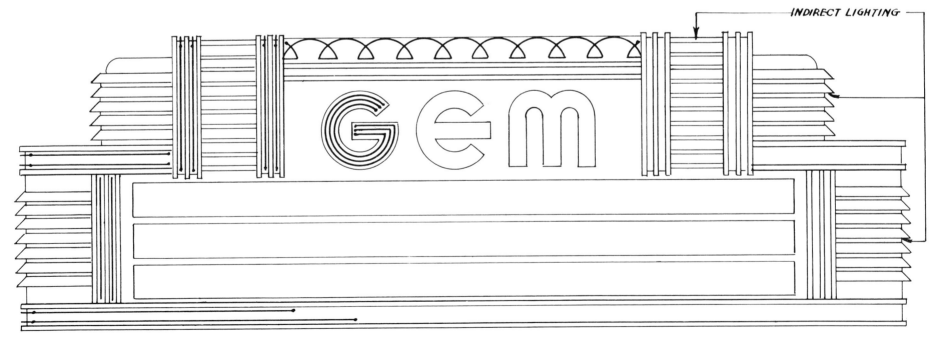

INDIRECT LIGHTING

PLATE 66

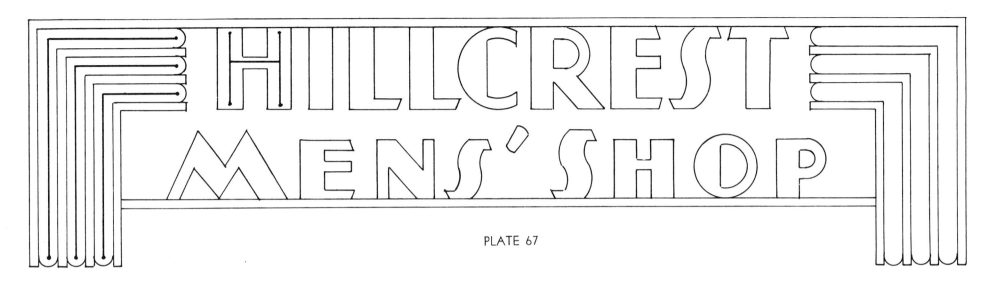

HILLCREST
MENS' SHOP

PLATE 67

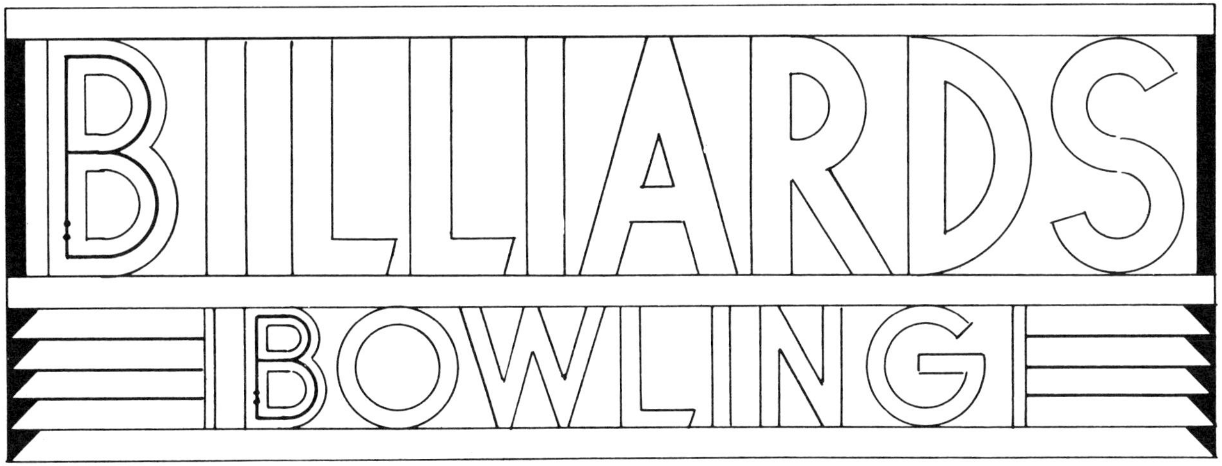

BILLIARDS
BOWLING

PLATE 68

PLATE 69

PLATE 70

PLATE 71

PLATE 72

PLATE 73

PLATE 74

PLATE 75

PLATE 76

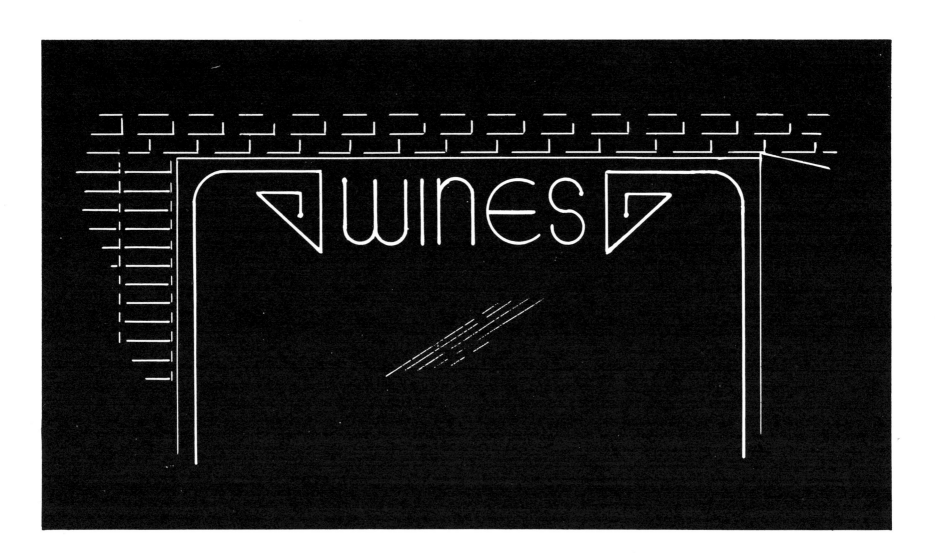

PLATE 77

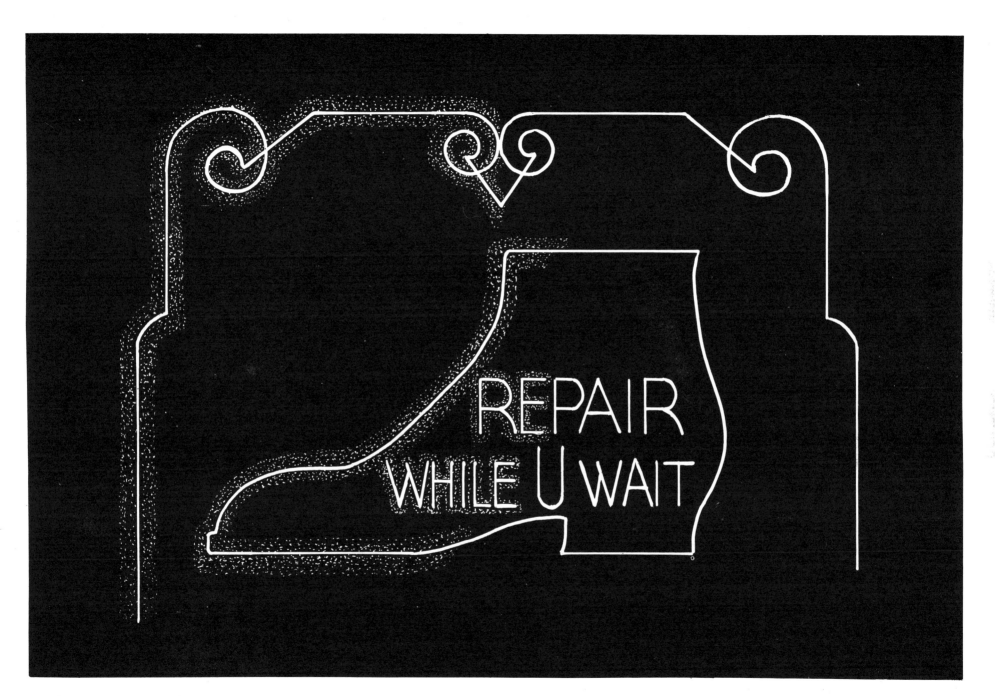

PLATE 78

PLATE 79

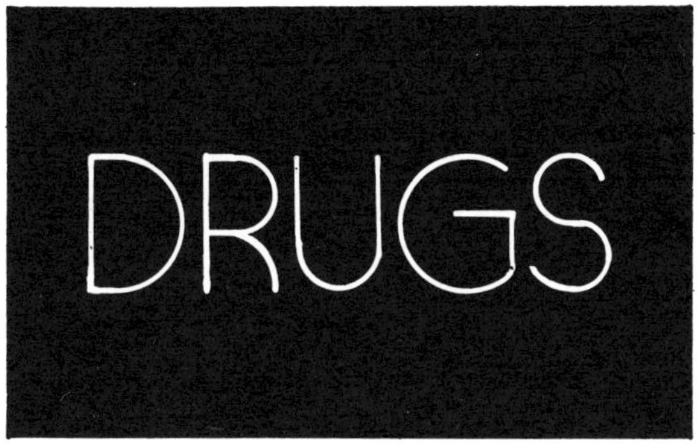

DRUGS

PLATE 80

CANDY

PLATE 81

SODA

PLATE 82

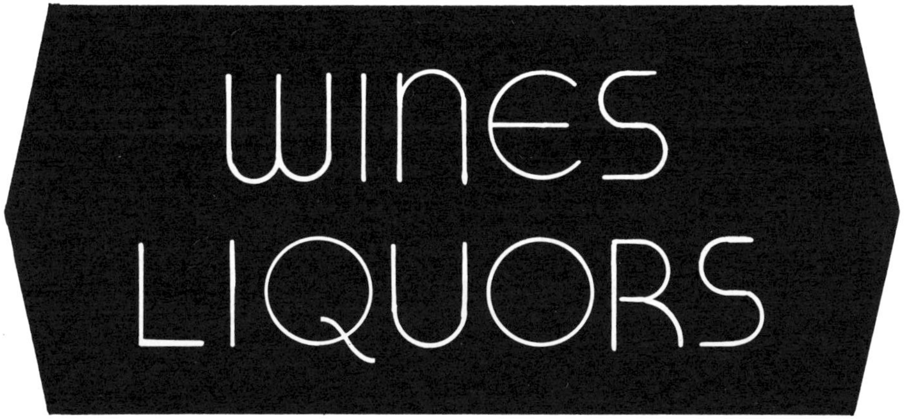

WINES
LIQUORS

PLATE 83

Cut-Rate
COSMETICS

PLATE 84

BEER

PLATE 85

CIGARS

PLATE 86

BAR

PLATE 87

AUTO
REPAIRS

PLATE 88

AUTO
GLASS

PLATE 89

BATTERIES

PLATE 90

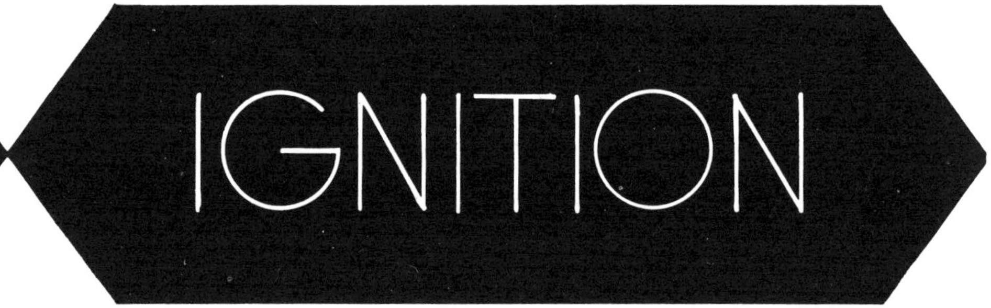

IGNITION

PLATE 91

USED
CARS

PLATE 92

AUTO
SUPPLIES

PLATE 93

PLATE 94

PLATE 95

PLATE 96

Prescriptions

PLATE 97

PLATE 98

PLATE 99

PLATE 100

PLATE 101

PLATE 102

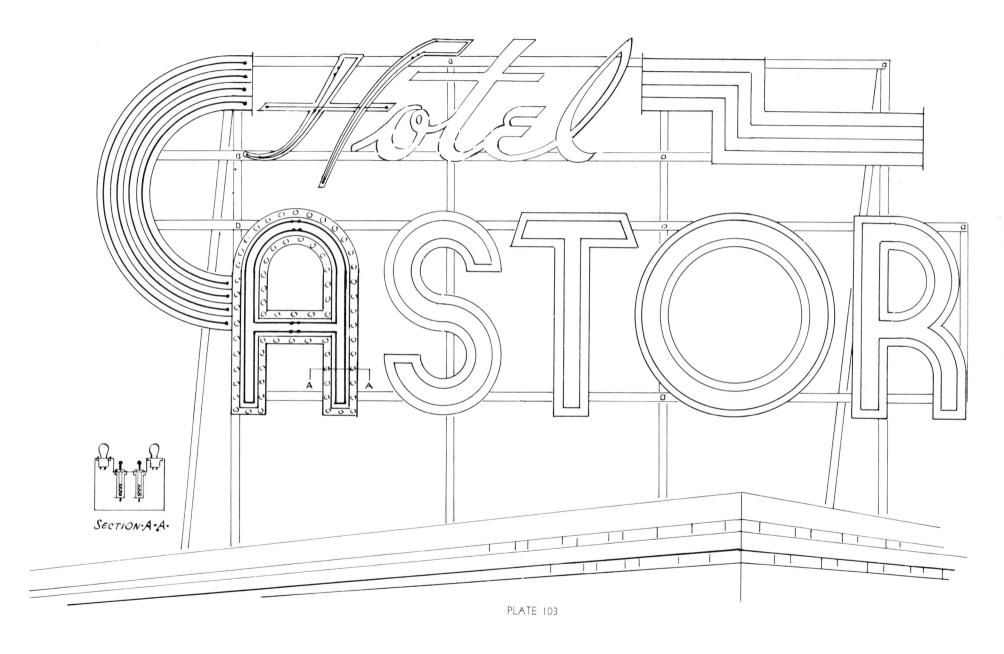

Hotel CASTOR

SECTION·A·A·

PLATE 103

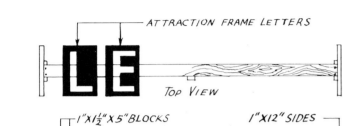

ATTRACTION FRAME LETTERS

TOP VIEW

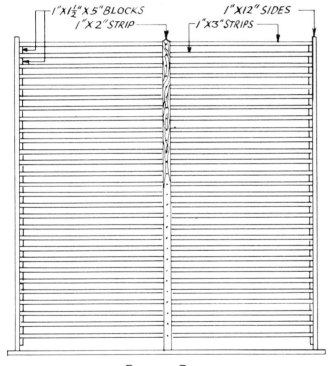

1"X1½"X5"BLOCKS

1"X2"STRIP

1"X12"SIDES

1"X3"STRIPS

DRYING RACK

PLATE 108

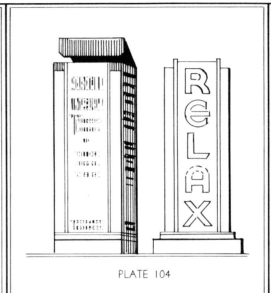

PLATE 104

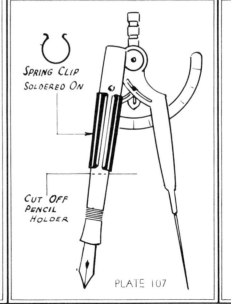

SPRING CLIP
SOLDERED ON

CUT OFF
PENCIL
HOLDER

PLATE 107

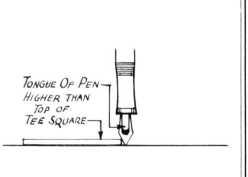

TONGUE OF PEN
HIGHER THAN
TOP OF
TEE SQUARE

PLATE 106

PLATE 105

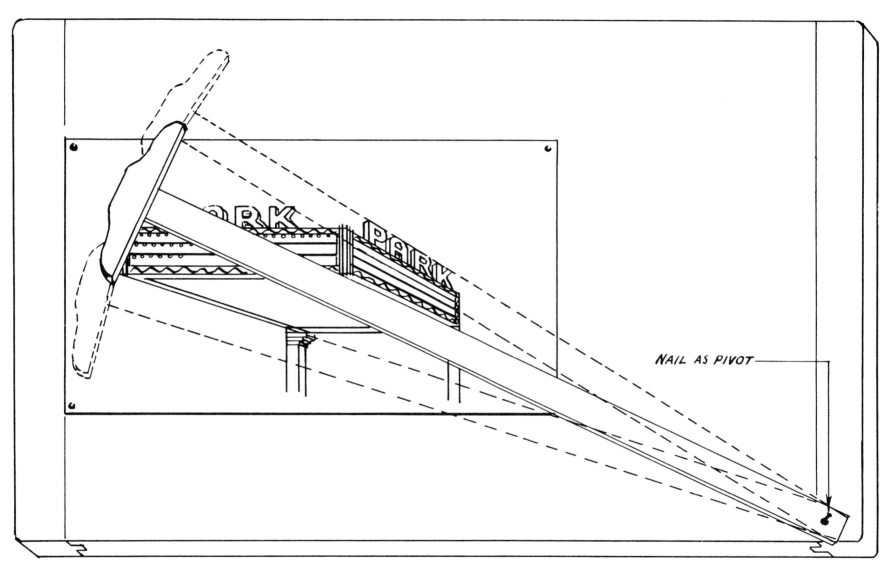

NAIL AS PIVOT

PIVOT POINT PERSPECTIVE

PLATE 109

INDEX TO PLATES

INDEX TO PLATES

INDEX TO CHAPTERS

LUMINOUS ADVERTISING SKETCHES BOOK NO. 2

A NEW AIM   A TONIC FOR THE SIGN INDUSTRY

Electrical advertising, combined with its many branches, is rated as one of America's largest industries. It is the very life blood of every firm. Every business is built on advertising.

To realize the vastness and power of electrical advertising, and the important role it plays in carrying the message home to the buying public, you must consider the many different techniques used to attract attention, promote sales, and improve business conditions. Observe the outstanding beauty of artistic designs and color displayed in many of the modern electrical advertising creations. Taking advantage of the latest display ideas with an excellent choice of the high grade materials available, the advertising power of the large spectacular electrical displays with gigantic letters and pictorials is tremendous. To mention some of the types, there are thousands of bulletins and identification signs which flash on and off. Signs that spell, animated cartoons and pictorials in lamps and neon, traveling message signs, illuminated structural outlining and decorating that vibrate with light, color and action. When these are considered together, they add up to the reason why electrical advertising is one of the best advertising mediums of the day.

Illuminated signs and displays play a part in the lives of everyone of us. Strangers in a town usually consider the center of the town and activity where they see the greatest massing of illuminated advertising signs. Can you picture a business section or highway or the GREAT WHITE WAY of New York or any other town, without an illuminated sign? A mental picture of such an impossible calamity, to me, would be the nearest thing to a ghost town.

Imagine driving along a highway for about fifty miles, without seeing a sign. It would soon become monotonous. Nature is wonderful in every season of the year, but reading road signs are interesting and enlightening.

Since the introduction of the modern trend and of many new materials which are advantagious to the sign industry, beautiful signs and modern fronts have become a necessity and are demanded by the merchants in all localities.

The many changes required to modernize old store fronts and signs, the altering of theatre fronts and marquees to the more modern designs, offer many opportunities for profitable business. With these known facts in view, it remains in the hands of the sales executives of every sign and advertising firm to get this business. But, do not stop here. The objective is to create more sign work. Many merchants and business men are so busy with their own individual work that they do not have the time to think of the unattractive appearance of their store fronts or other sign work which may be required. To sell a sign to a business man who knows he needs a sign, is the simplest form of salesmanship and is the usual routine method that the sign salesman uses in closing deals. This method of doing business is not enough and is not becoming to the sign industry and its purpose. It leaves virtually untapped the big profits which are derived in any field from creative selling.

The average sign firm just builds signs and forgets the original purpose of their business, the most outstanding factor that their business should be built on, and that is to realize that they are fundamentally ADVERTISERS and subsequently builders of advertising materials.

Now as advertisers, their duty is to create and originate advertising possibilities. To discover new locations, spots or shots, meaning a position or place where a sign can be erected, giving the greatest possible advertising value per dollar to the buyer.

If a business man has a sign or two on his store front, it does not necessarily mean that he is not a live sign prospect. The good advertiser can see many possibilities for rendering service or selling another sign. Look the job over thoroughly. More signs may be needed. The modernizing of a store front may make a new modern sign desirable if not absolutely necessary. Repainting or rehanging of a sign to a better position on a building, or new modern window signs to make his place look smart and in keeping with the times, may be required.

We would like to suggest a practical system which past experience has shown can be employed with satisfactory results. The salesman, in this instance, makes the first move in visualizing new advertising possibilities, which promising firms can use, and submit their ideas to the prospect. This can be realized by first taking a camera shot of a prospective location, building or store front. Get this picture enlarged (known as a photographic blowup). Combine your ideas with your shop designer and super-impose thereon your sign designs, making a beautiful composition of what the actual finished signs and front will look like on completion. In submitting this photographic blowup, the customer has before him the picture of his store front or building, plus the signs that you feel will interest and give him the most advertising value. Having won his confidence, the next step is to explain the advantage gained through the use of your proposed signs and displays.

The sign salesman must sell advertising value, plus signs. He must therefore be a pioneer and advertising advisor to business men. Doctors help a sick person and advise them how to keep fit and well. Sign salesmen can help a poor business grow or a good business increase their volume of sales by advising or prescribing the use of the proper type of electrical advertising signs. A sign salesman cannot close a sign contract without submitting to a prospective customer a sign design or plan of proposed work. Therefore, the more sketches submitted to prospects, the more possibility of getting orders. To keep things humming, keep the sign design department busy and the sign industry will prosper.

In proposing sign suggestions, designs, etc. a good quality for salesmen and designers to possess is to be able to recognize the limitation of a design or suggestion of same, so that you stay well within the financial means of the purchaser. The modern trend of sign designing eliminates many useless frills and scrolls (gingerbread and cheesecake) used a decade ago. Modern designs are made up of simple lines and massive background spaces. Useless copy is eliminated. The less reading matter on a sign, the better for reading at a glance. This has the advantage of being read, understood, and keeps pace with this fast moving era.

Sign designs that are well executed along modern lines, properly colored, not necessarily elaborate, but containing the most advertising value, make a good impression and sell upon presentation to prospective buyers.

SINGING A WORD OF PRAISE

TO SALESMEN

Selling is the motivating power behind the sign industry. Thousands of dollars are invested in this industry and business depends on the salesmen to make these investments pay a higher dividend. Realizing this fact, an increase in the volume of business can be tactfully planned.

Rarely do you see or hear of a man who goes out on his own accord to buy insurance. Insurance is sold to you in your home, in your office, in the subway, or in a plane while you are standing, sitting or walking. Time and place mean nothing to the insurance salesman. He is fully prepared to sell you just the right type of a policy, you need and the kind that you can afford, according to your means and income. He is prepared to do business at all times. His briefcase contains the answers to all questions fired at him and he can close a deal on his first call in many instances. Insurance companies flourish through these methods and are not interrupted by hard times, depressions, or recessions. Every territory is thoroughly covered and canvassed. Every living person is their prospect and they seek you out from Little America to the North Pole, also chase you around the equator if necessary to get you to sign on the dotted line. To get this business, they know they need plenty of good trained salesmen. Now apply this method directly to the sign industry and you can be assured of a thriving and a lucrative sign industry.

FROM BEAUTIFUL SKETCHES

LARGE SIGN PLANTS GROW

The sign industry of today must at least double the number of their sales force. Salesmen should be known and act as advertising agents to every prospect. To achieve any marked degree of success, the employers of sign shops should cooperate fully with their salesmen, supplying them with plenty of sketches.

Good salesmen make business pay profits, and they, in return, should receive adequate compensation. Employers should encourage new and young blood to get into this lucrative business, train them and devise some financial means to keep them on the job. This exciting field can provide the satisfactions that come from visualizing, creating, and then finally seeing your ideas take material form.

In composing this second portfolio of "Luminous Advertising Sketches" the sole purpose is to create more sales. To do this, I have set a goal before me, to design signs that will appeal to practically all merchants.

Designing of electrical signs is an art, and I have endeavored to bring out both the full artistic and commercial values combined. Inexpensive displays with the most catchy designs and plenty of advertising punch—not elaborate or fantastic.

Equip your salesmen with a copy of "Luminous Advertising Sketches" and they will be prepared to do business with any prospect on the spot, as this modern sketch book contains many practical designs which are adaptable to almost any type of establishment.

Book No. 2

LUMINOUS ADVERTISING SKETCHES

PHILIP DILEMME

A TREATISE ON • ELECTRIC SIGNS

• STORE FRONT DESIGNS

• ABSTRACTS OF MODERN

• ALPHABETS

REFLECTED
PLAN of SOFFIT

PLATE 110

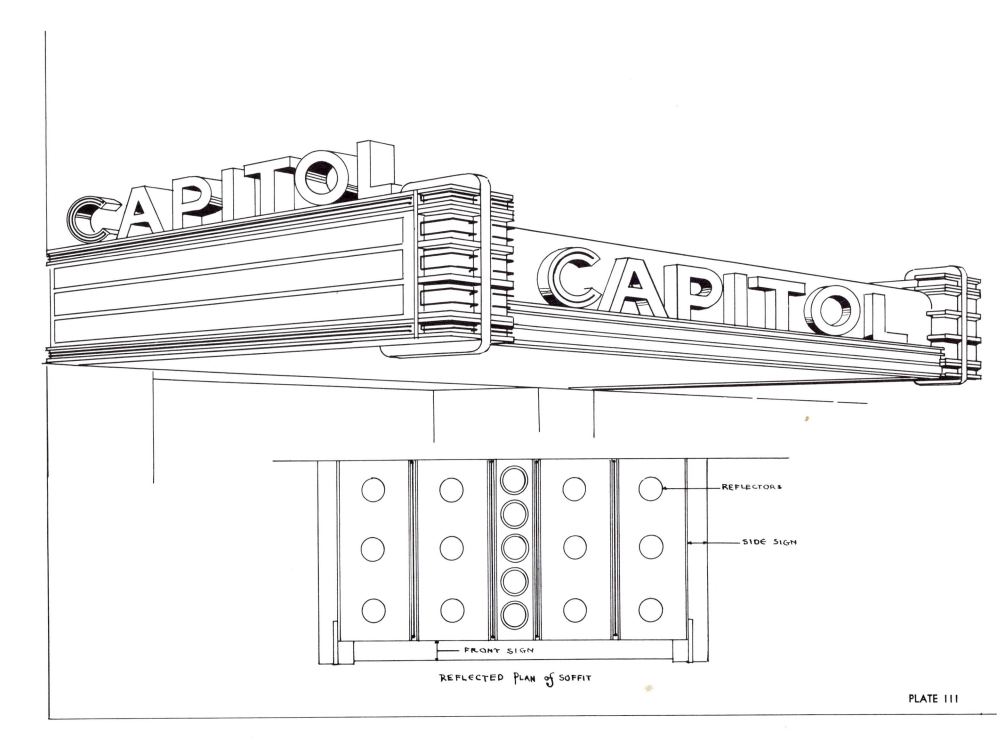

REFLECTORS

SIDE SIGN

FRONT SIGN

REFLECTED PLAN of SOFFIT

PLATE III

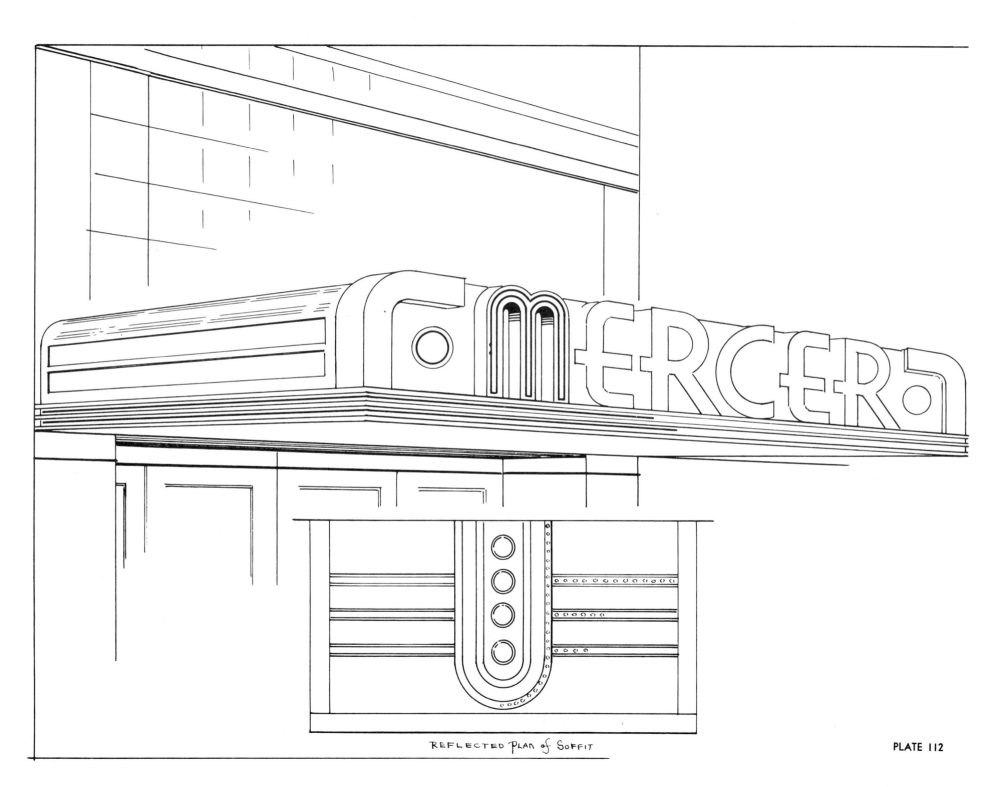

REFLECTED PLAN of SOFFIT

PLATE 112

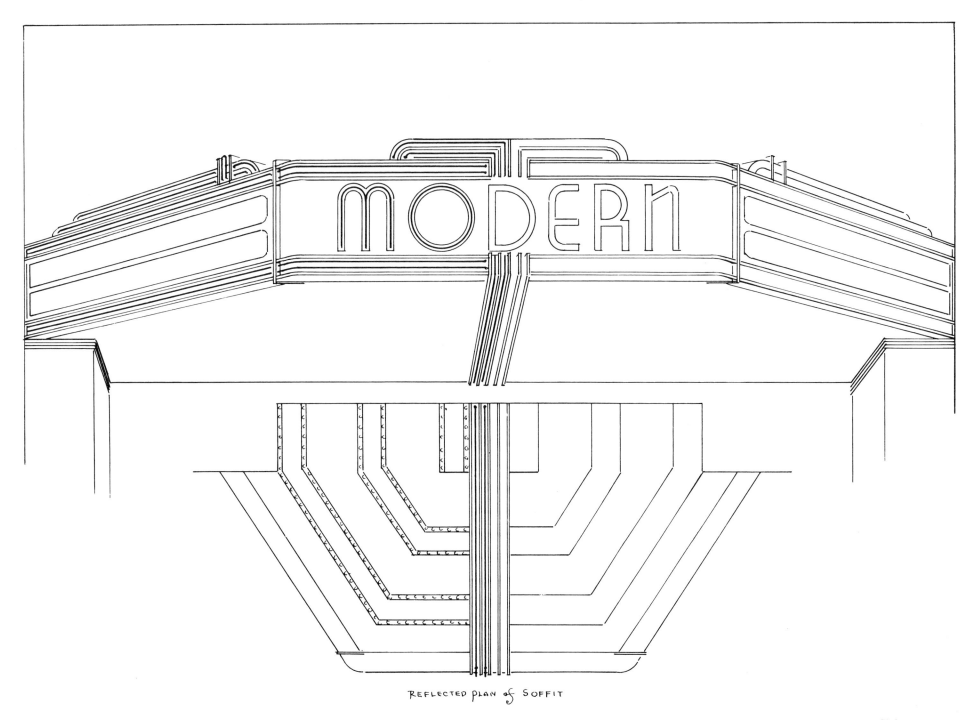

REFLECTED PLAN of SOFFIT

PLATE 113

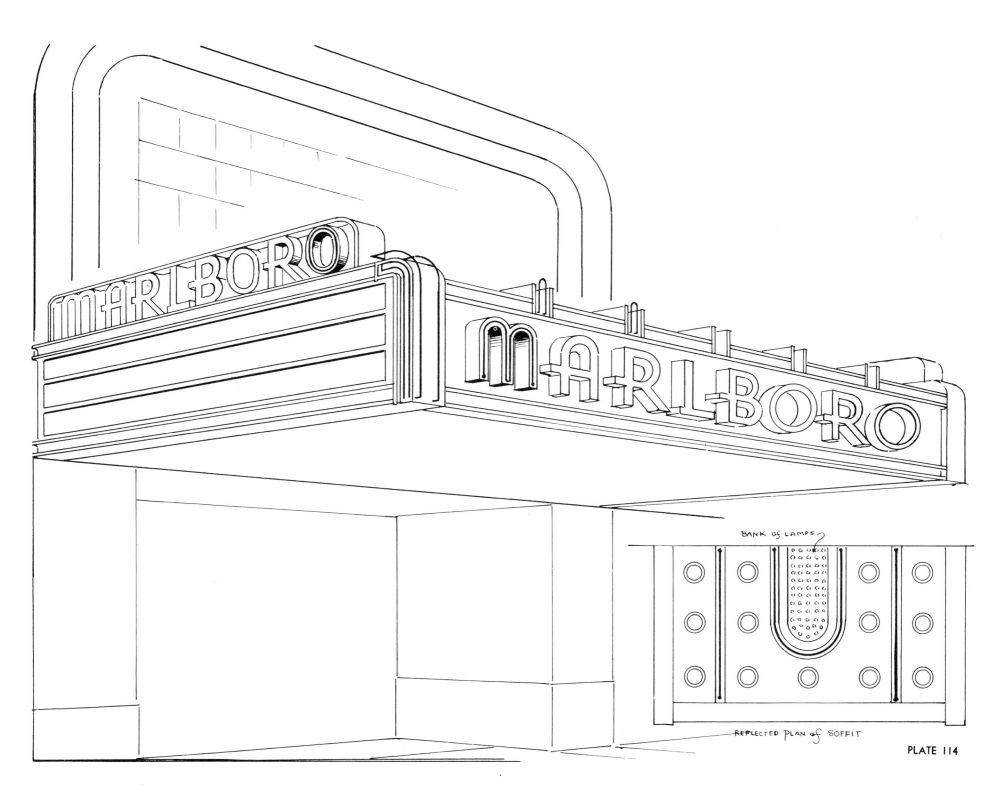

BANK OF LAMPS

REFLECTED PLAN OF SOFFIT

PLATE 114

PLATE 115

ASTOR

ASTOR

NEON

PLAN of FRONT SIGN

PLATE 116

SIDE VIEW
of CORNER POST

RAND HOTEL

GRAND HOTEL

BLDG LINE

REFLECTED PLAN OF SOFFIT

PLATE 117

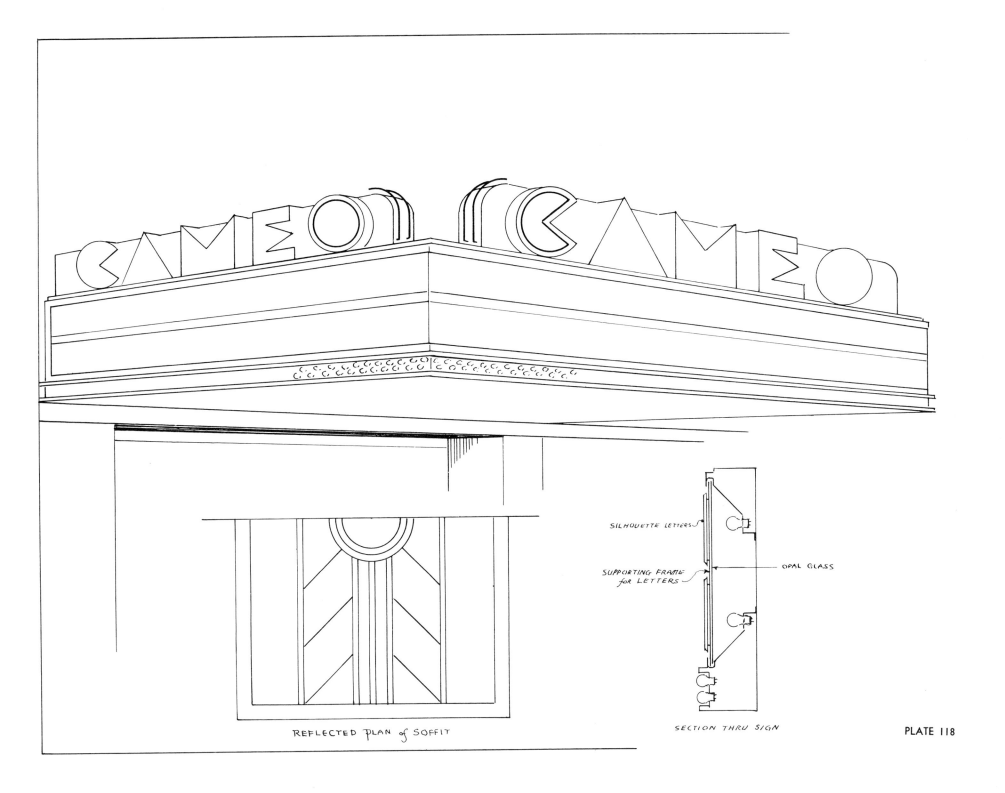

REFLECTED PLAN of SOFFIT

SILHOUETTE LETTERS

SUPPORTING FRAME for LETTERS

OPAL GLASS

SECTION THRU SIGN

PLATE 118

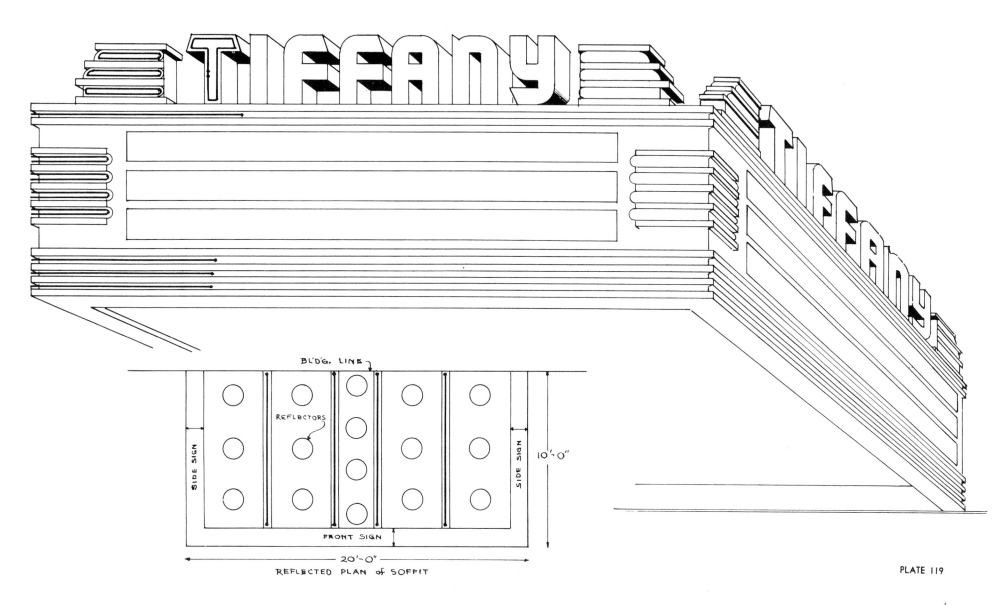

BLD'G. LINE

REFLECTORS

SIDE SIGN

SIDE SIGN

10'-0"

FRONT SIGN

20'-0"

REFLECTED PLAN of SOFFIT

PLATE 119

PLATE 121

PLATE 120

PLATE 122

PLATE 123

PLATE 125

PLAN

NEON

PLATE 124

PLAN

NEON

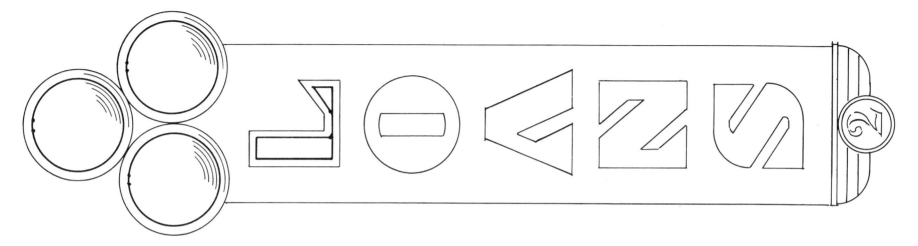

PLATE 127

PLATE 126

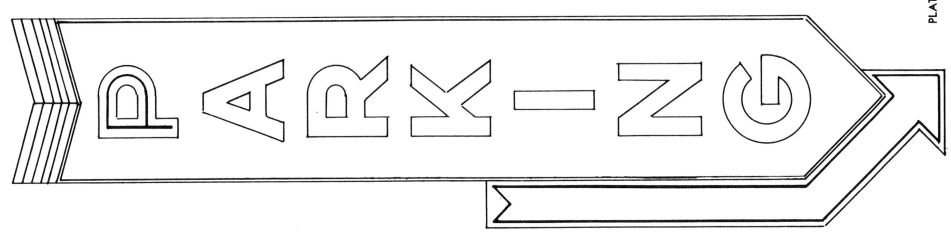

PLATE 129

PLATE 128

PLATE 131

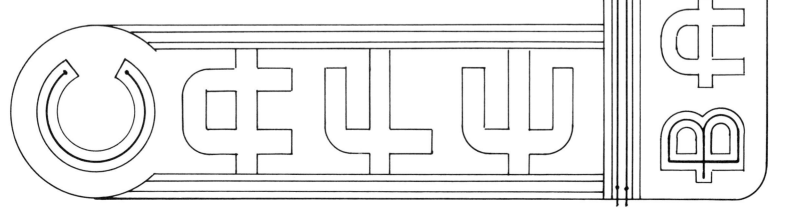

PLATE 130

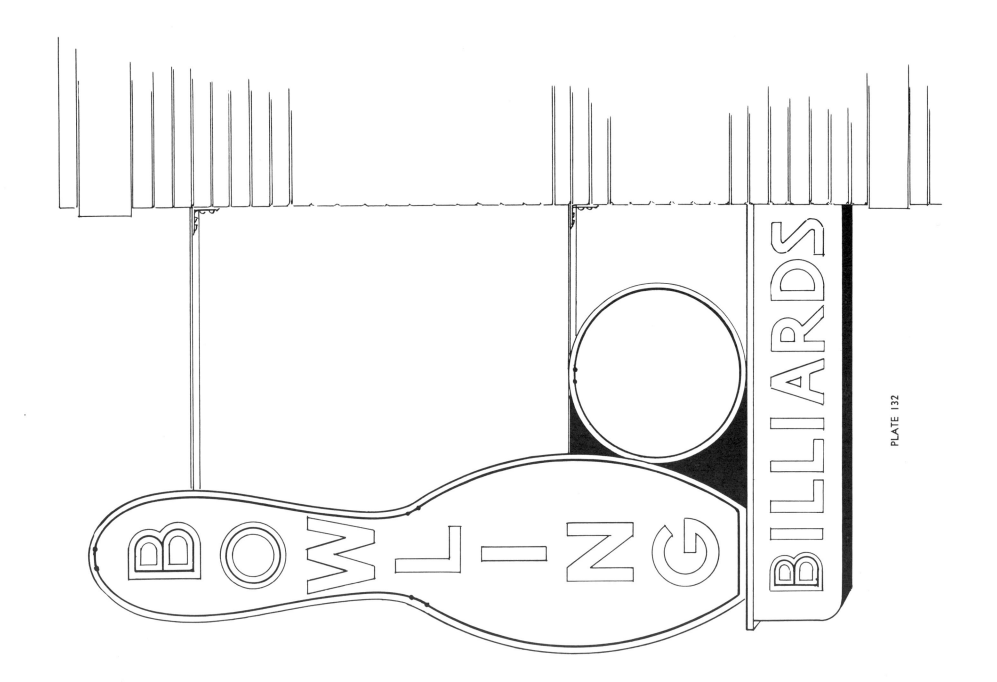

BILLIARDS

BOWLING

PLATE 132

PLATE 133

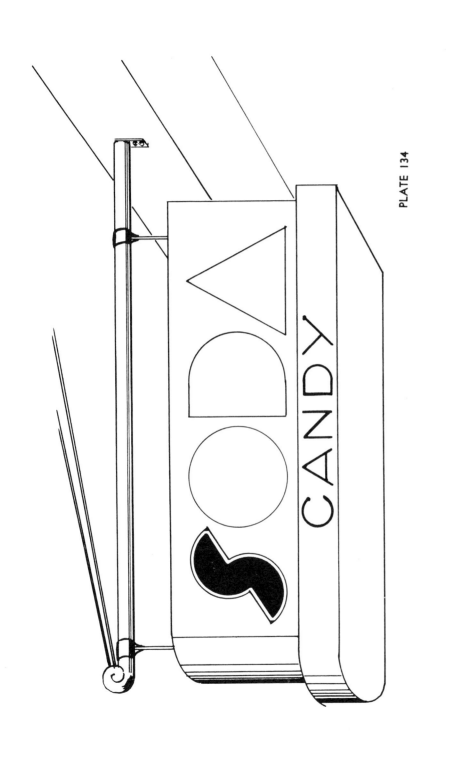

PLATE 134

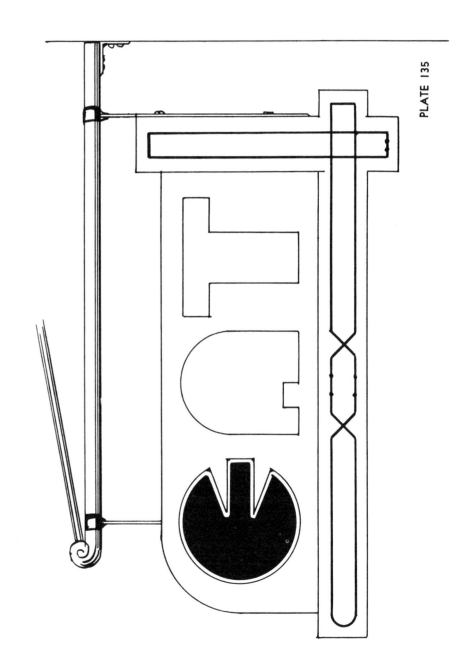

PLATE 135

LIMA
RADIO

PLATE 136

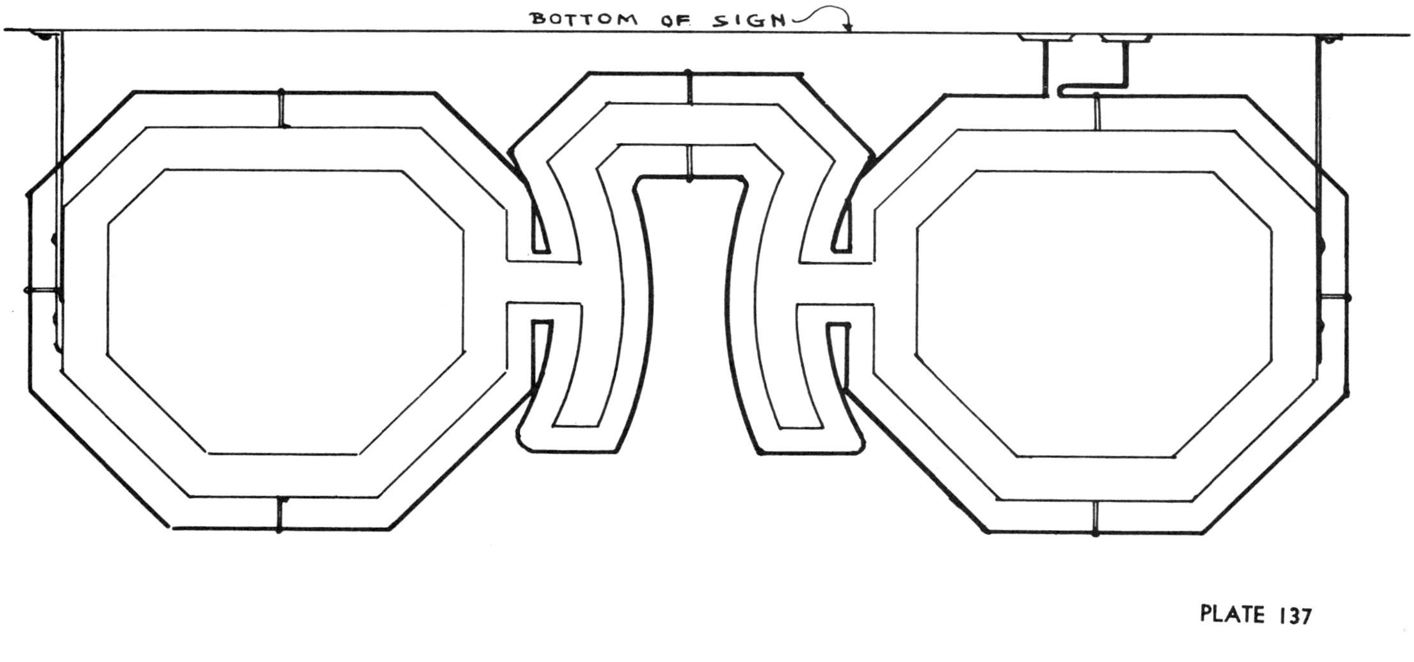

BOTTOM OF SIGN

PLATE 137

BEAUTY SALON

Rita

PLATE 138

PLATE 139

REPAIR

PLATE 140

YORKVILLE PORK

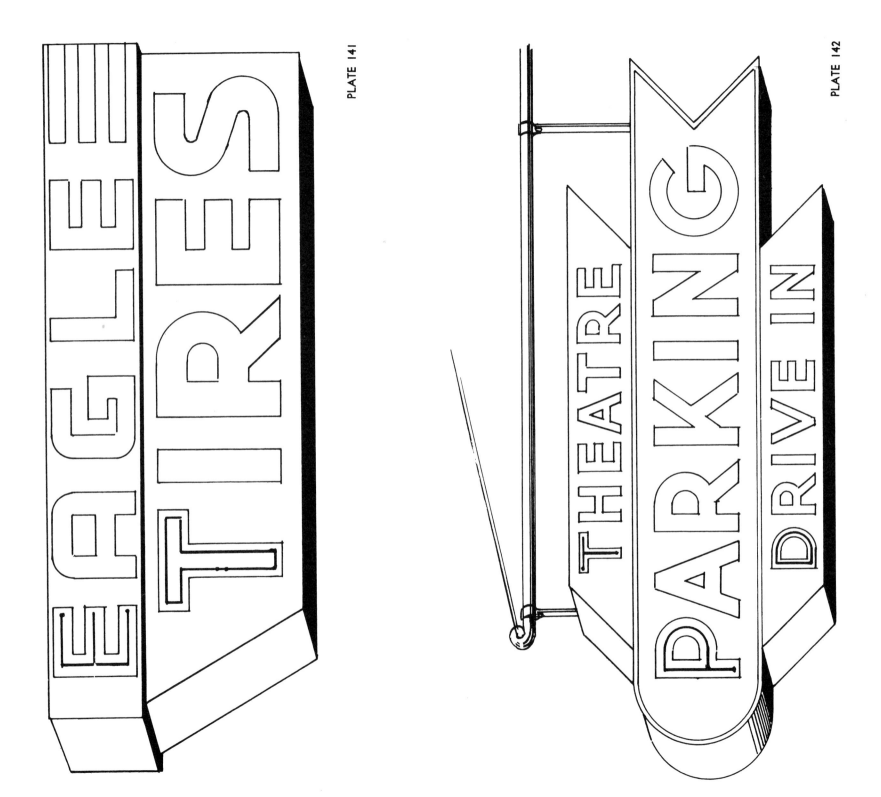

EAGLE TIRES

PLATE 141

THEATRE PARKING DRIVE IN

PLATE 142

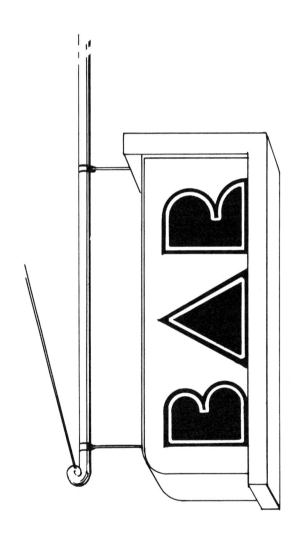

PLATE 143

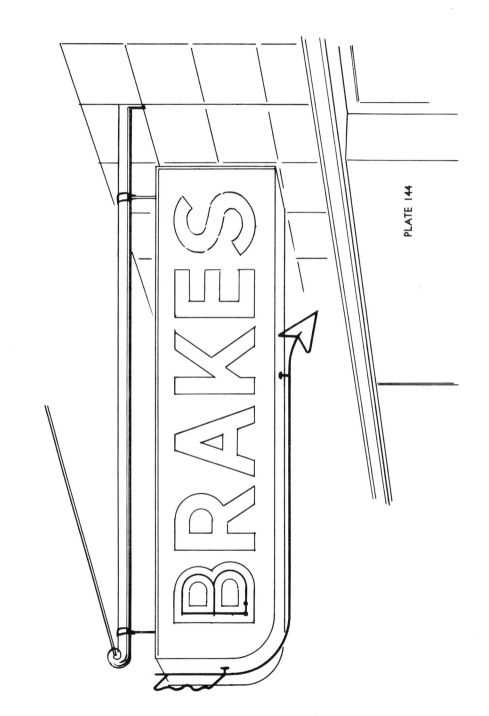

PLATE 144

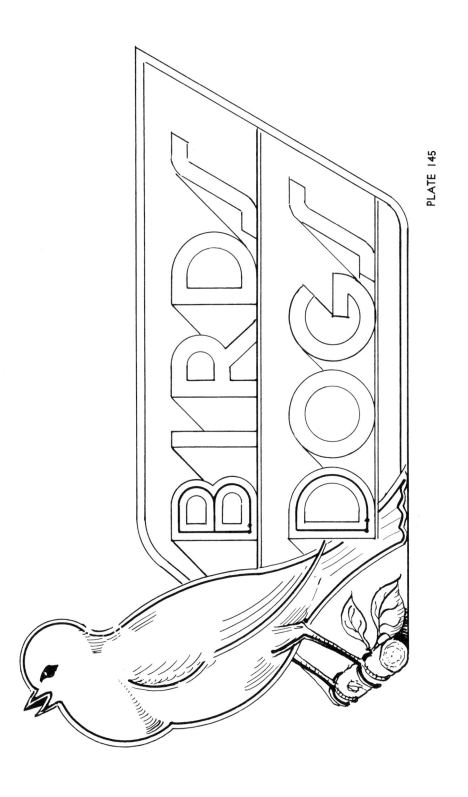

PLATE 145

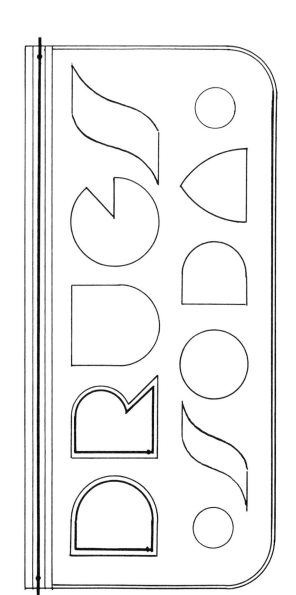

PLATE 146

BRACE

SKELETON NEON

NAME

PLATE 147

SECTION-A-A

PLATE 148

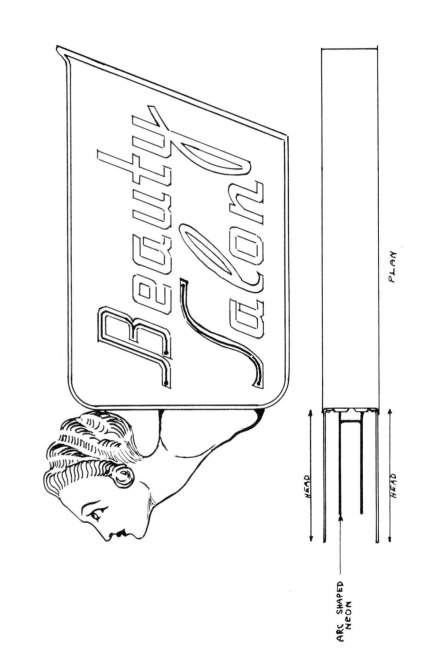

ARC SHAPED NEON

HEAD

HEAD

PLAN

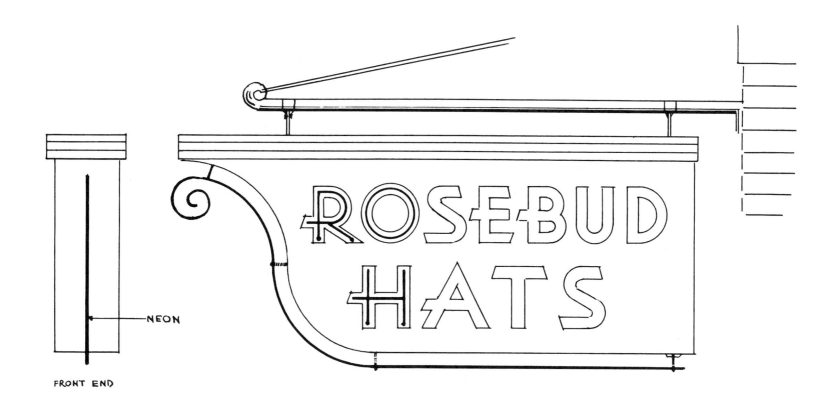

NEON

FRONT END

PLATE 150

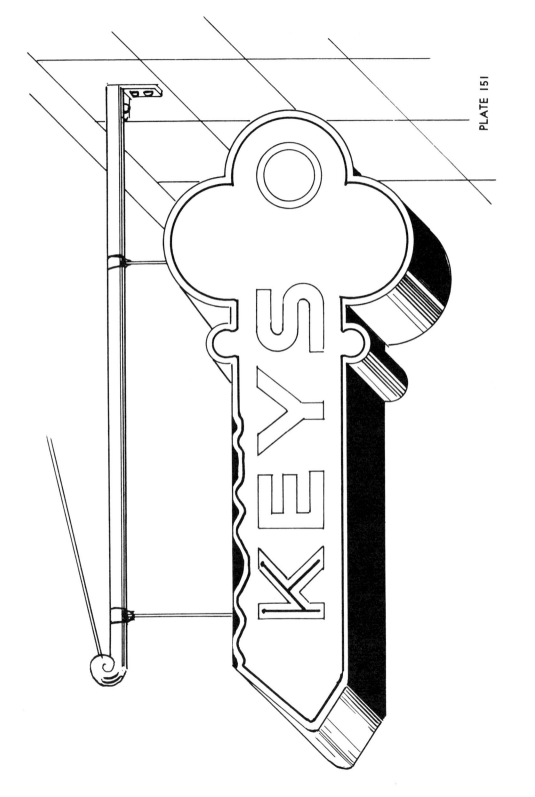

PLATE 151

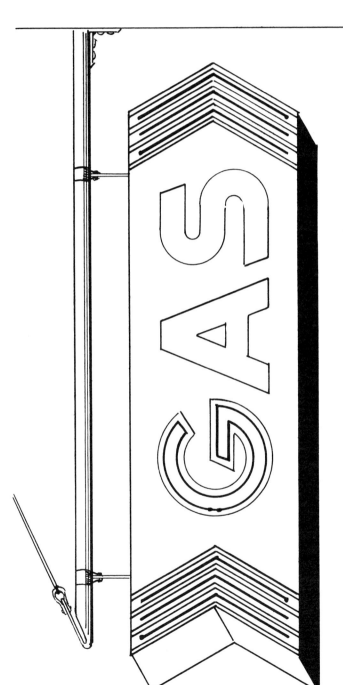

PLATE 152

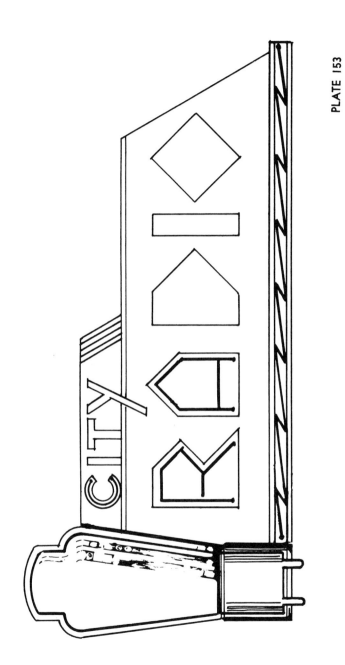

PLATE 153

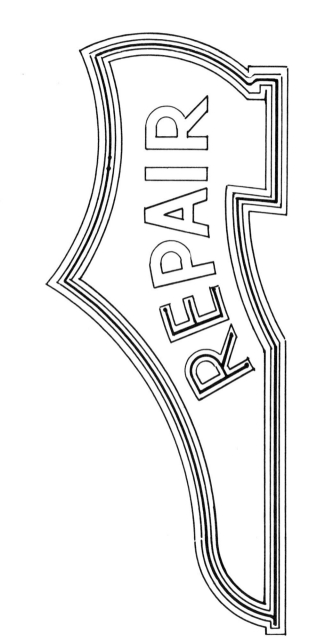

PLATE 154

PLATE 155

PLATE 156

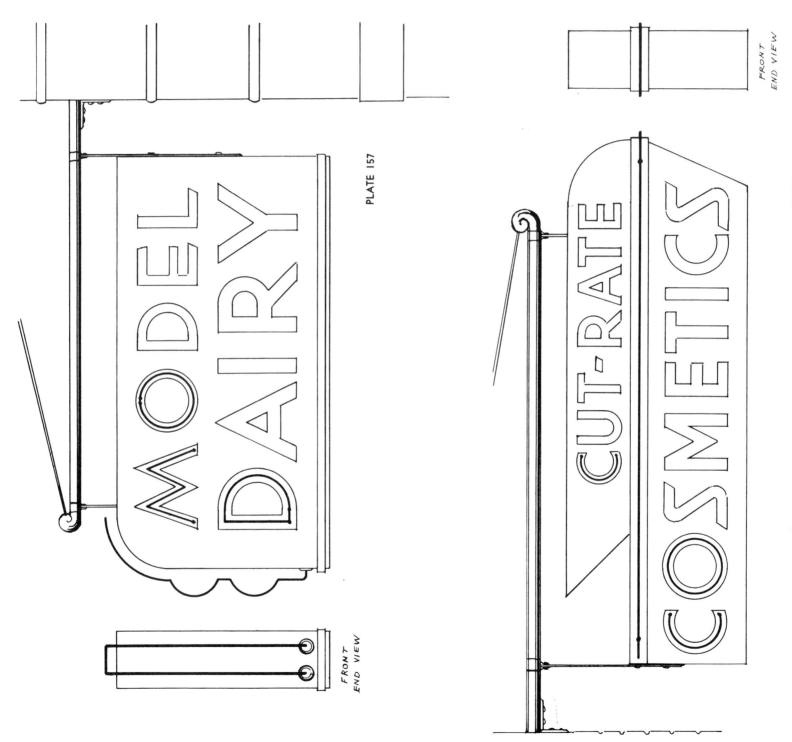

MODEL DAIRY

FRONT END VIEW

PLATE 157

CUT-RATE COSMETICS

FRONT END VIEW

PLATE 158

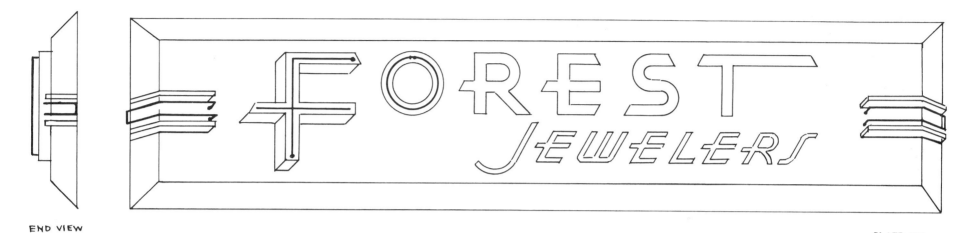

END VIEW

PLATE 159

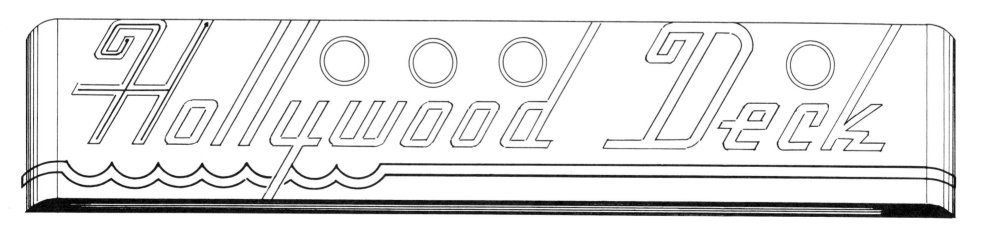

PLATE 160

TRIM

BLACK GLASS

CHANNEL LETTERS

NEON

SECTION THRU SIGN

BARONI'S

BEAUTY

SALON

PLATE 161

END VIEW

PLATE 162

PLATE 163

SECTION
THRU SIGN

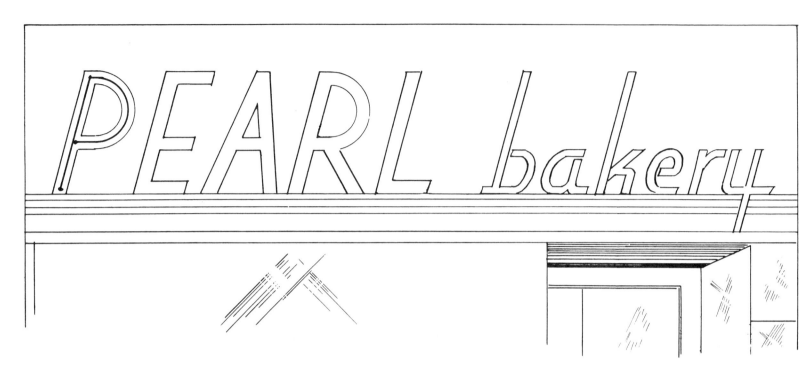

PLATE 164

PLATE 165

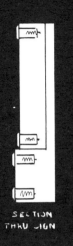

PARK club
BAR GRILL

SECTION
THRU SIGN

PLATE 166

LONG'S
SHIRT SHOP

SECTION
THRU SIGN

PLATE 167

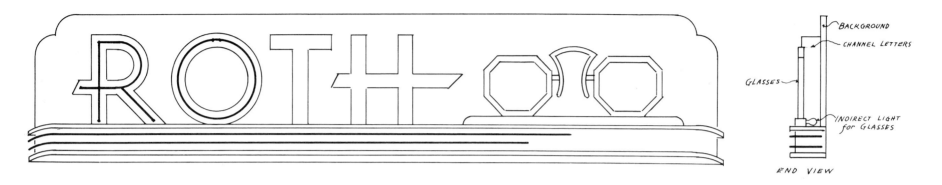

BACKGROUND
CHANNEL LETTERS
GLASSES
INDIRECT LIGHT
for GLASSES

END VIEW

PLATE 168

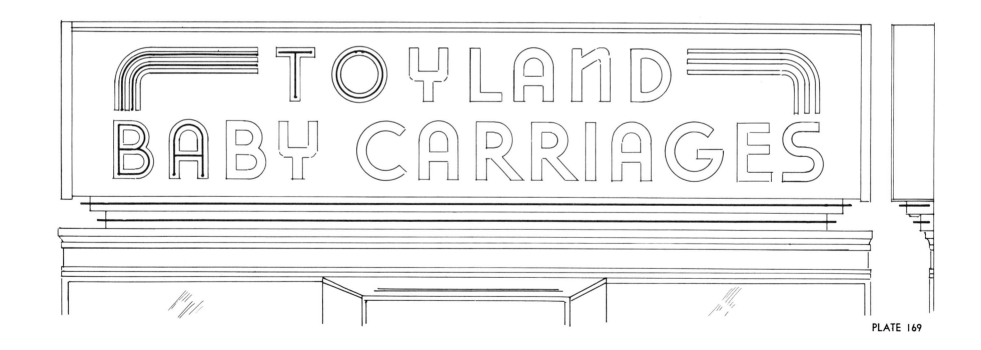

PLATE 169

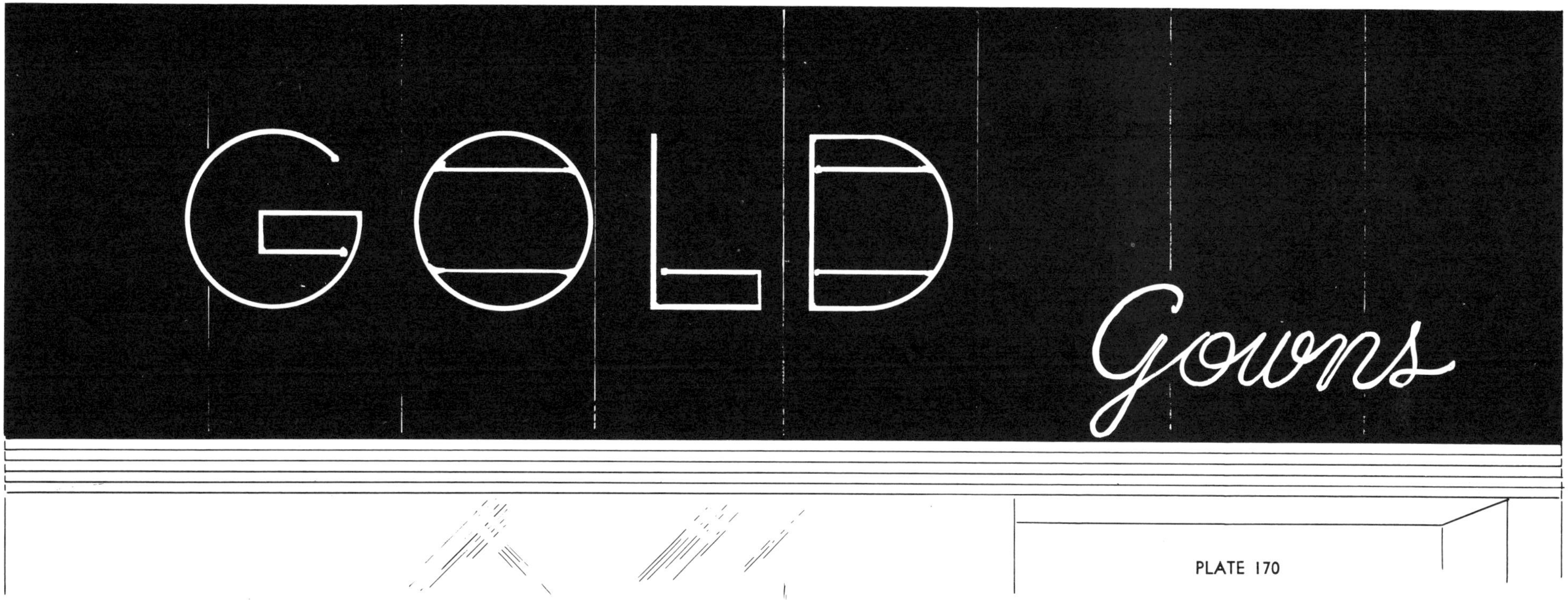

GOLD *Gowns*

PLATE 170

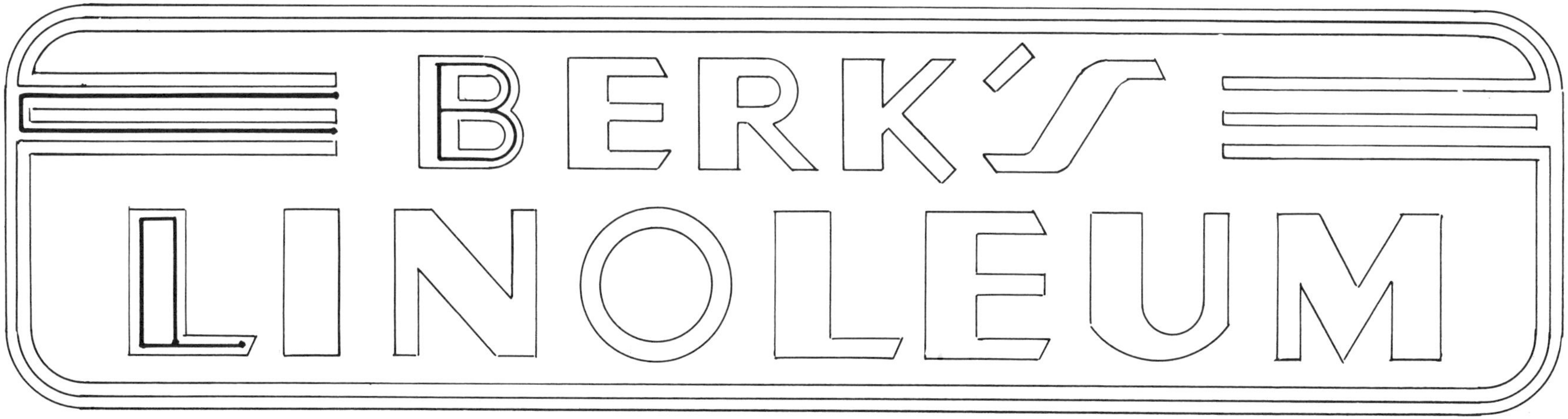

BERK'S LINOLEUM

PLATE 171

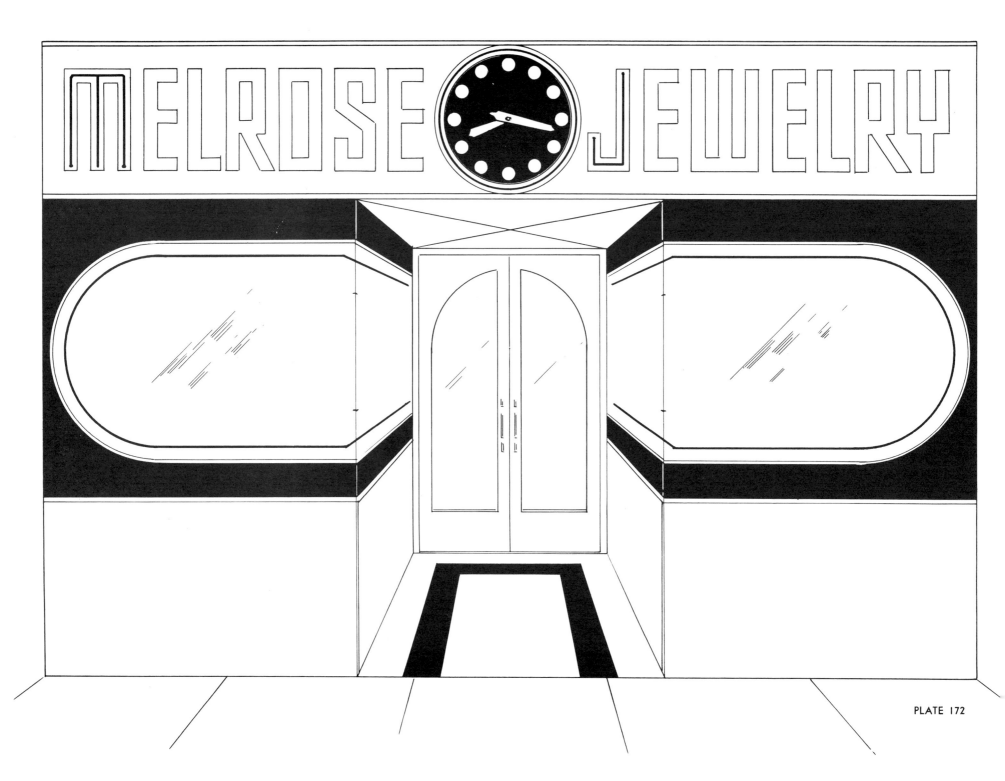

PLATE 172

PLATE 173

PLATE 174

SEA~FOOD

PLATE 175

PLATE 176

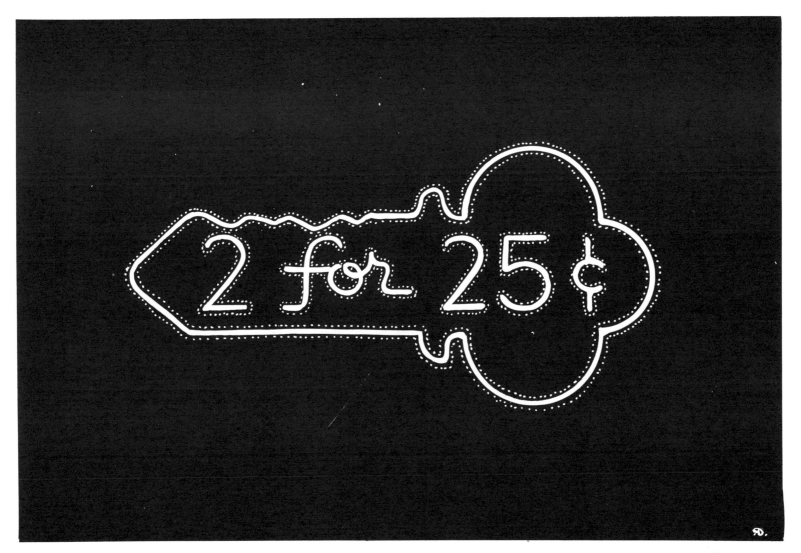

PLATE 177

PLATE 178

PLATE 179

PLATE 180

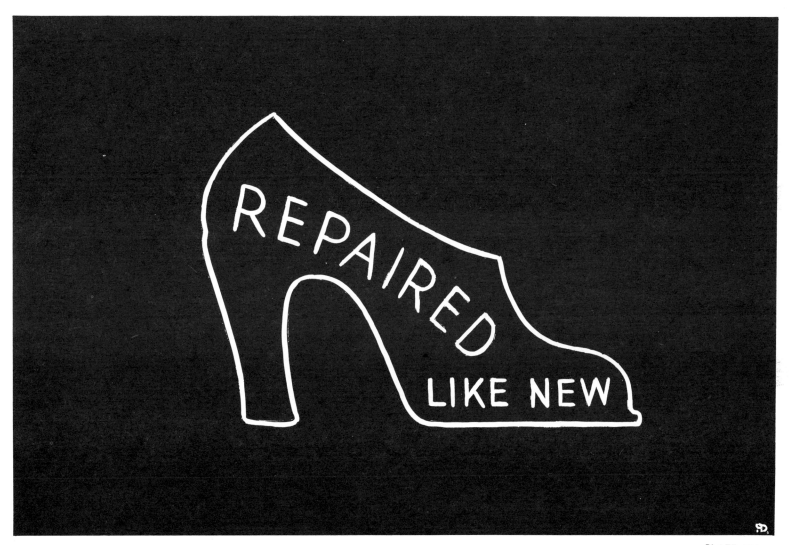

PLATE 181

PLATE 182

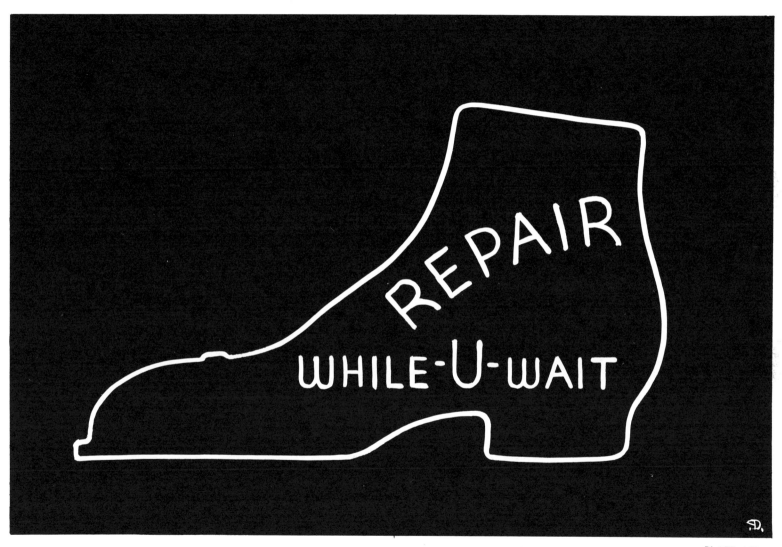

REPAIR
WHILE-U-WAIT

PLATE 183

Seafood

PLATE 184

Cocktails

PLATE 187

Quality MARKET

PLATE 185

DRUGS

PLATE 190

Cut Rate DRUGS

PLATE 188

LUNCHEON

PLATE 186

ICE CREAM

PLATE 189

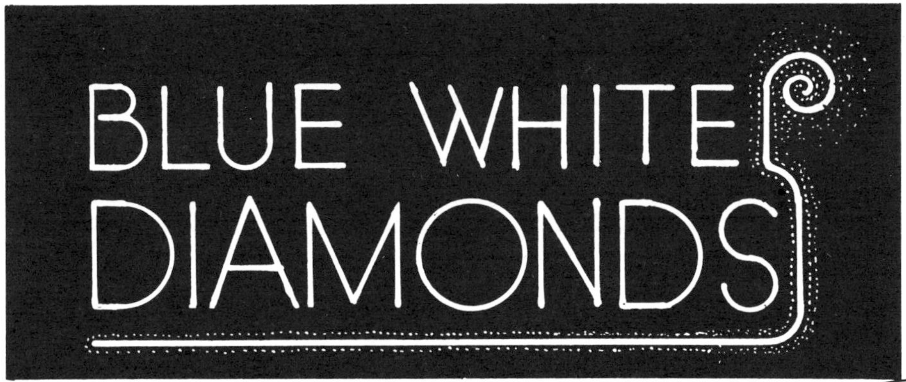
BLUE WHITE
DIAMONDS

PLATE 191

fine WATCH
REPAIRING

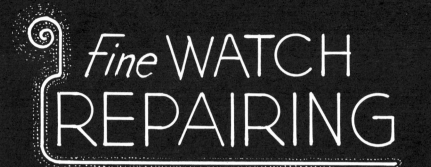

PLATE 194

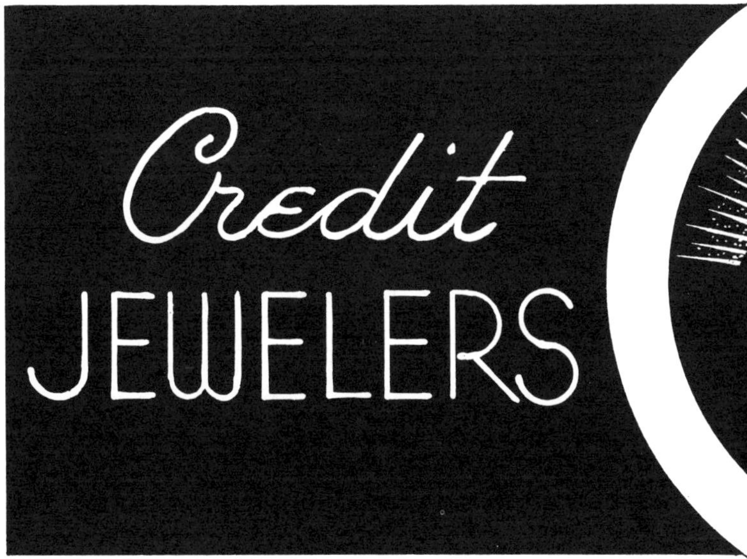
Credit
JEWELERS

PLATE 192

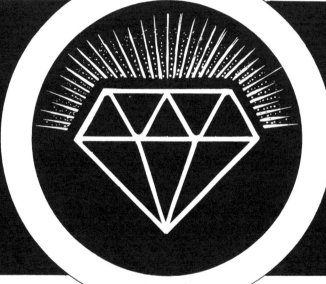

PLATE 197

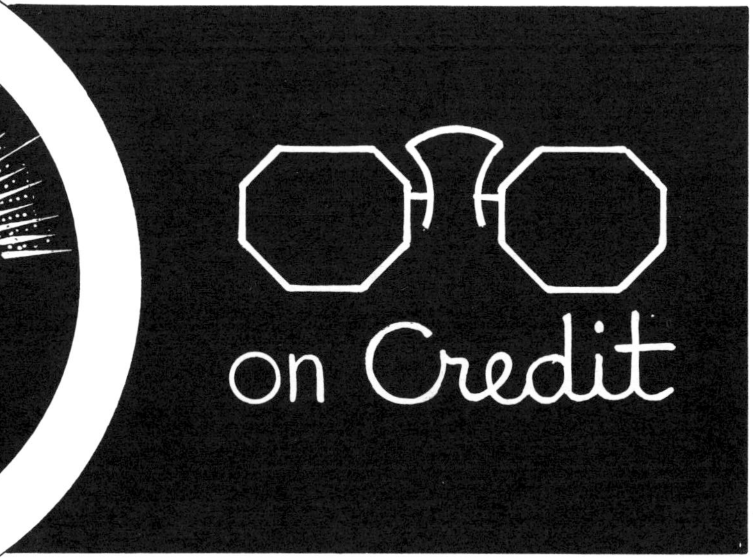
on Credit

PLATE 195

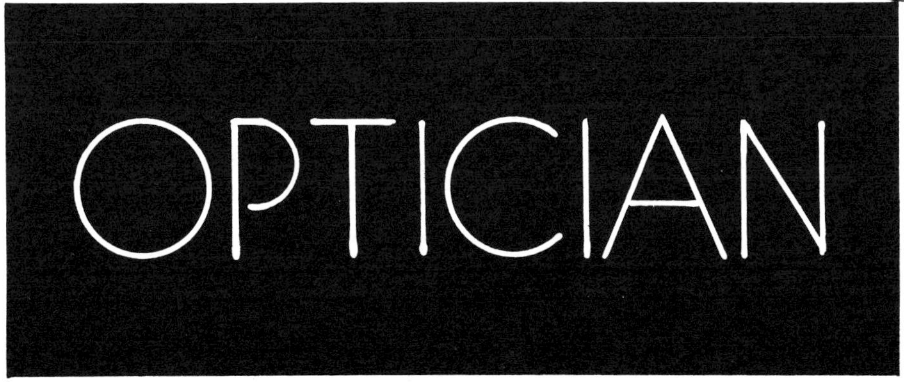
OPTICIAN

PLATE 193

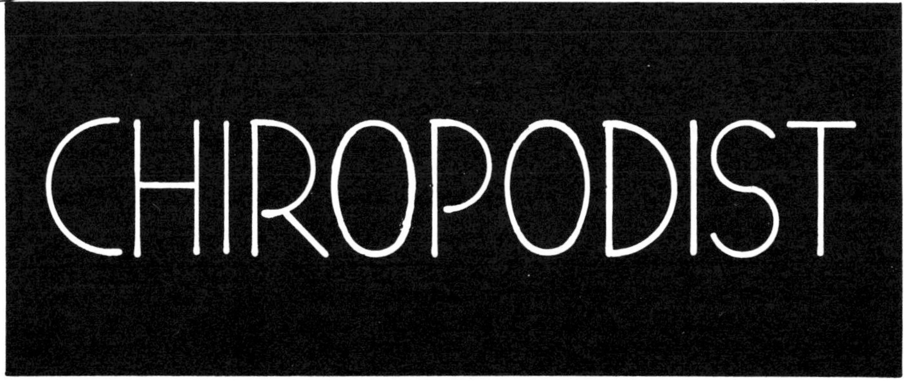
CHIROPODIST

PLATE 196

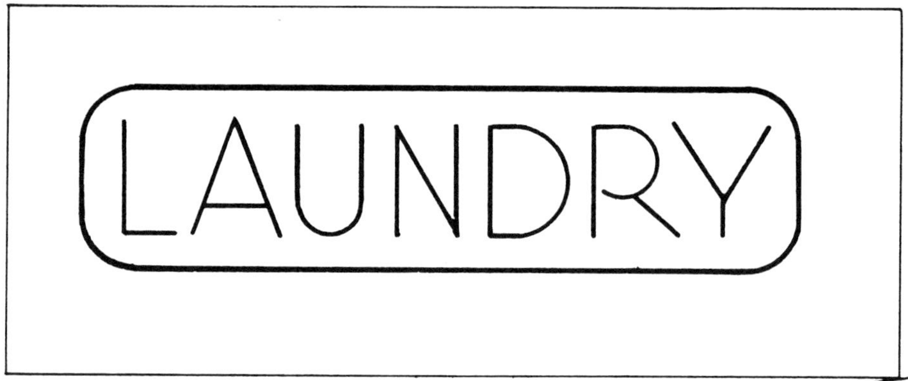

LAUNDRY

PLATE 198

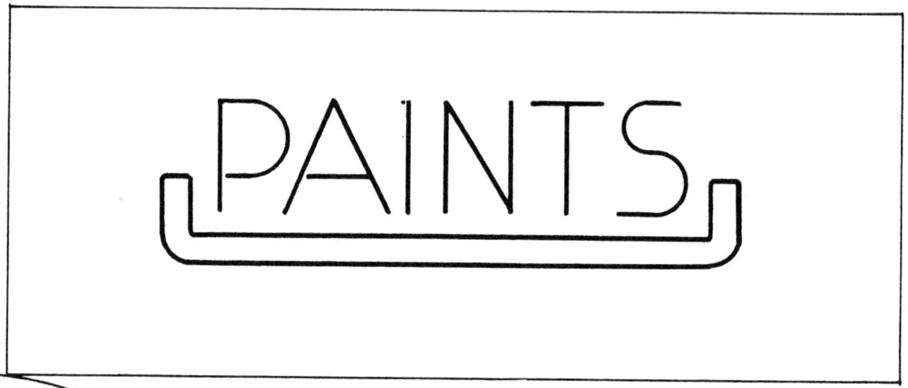

PAINTS

PLATE 201

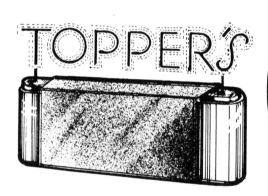

TOPPER'S

PLATE 199

FLORIST

PLATE 204

PERFUME

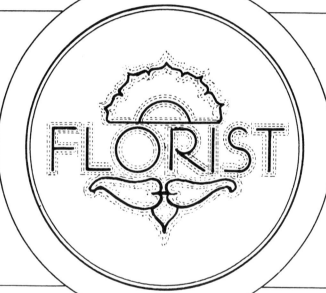

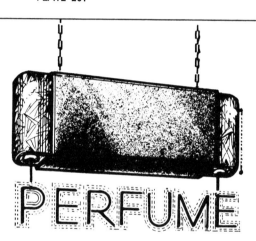

PLATE 202

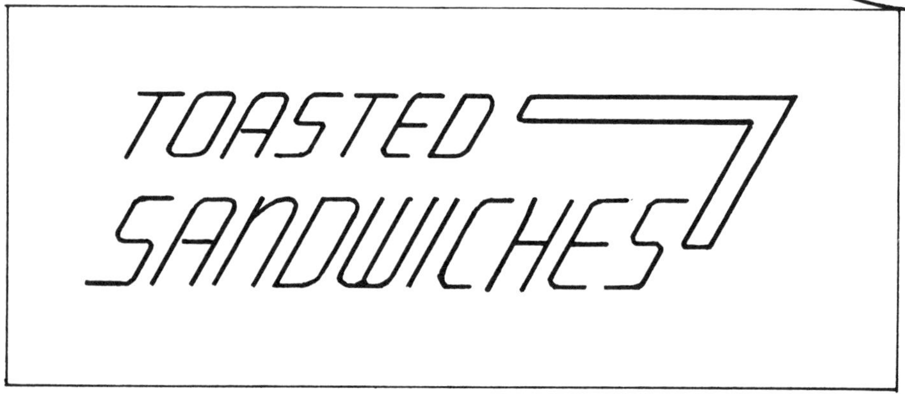

TOASTED
SANDWICHES

PLATE 200

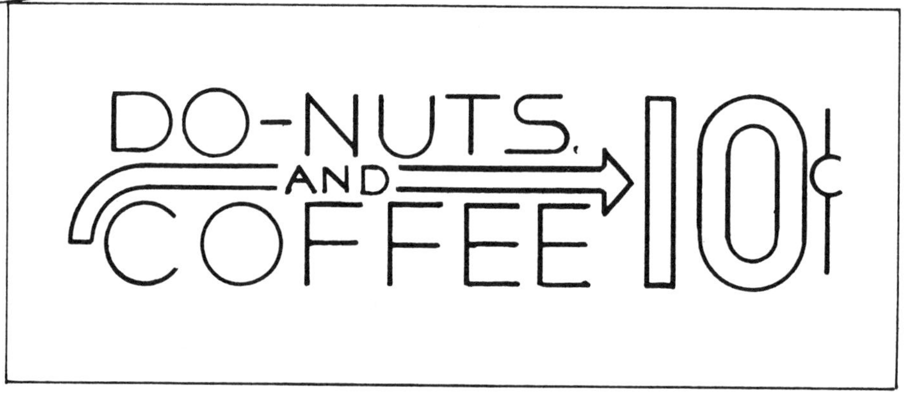

DO-NUTS
AND
COFFEE
10¢

PLATE 203

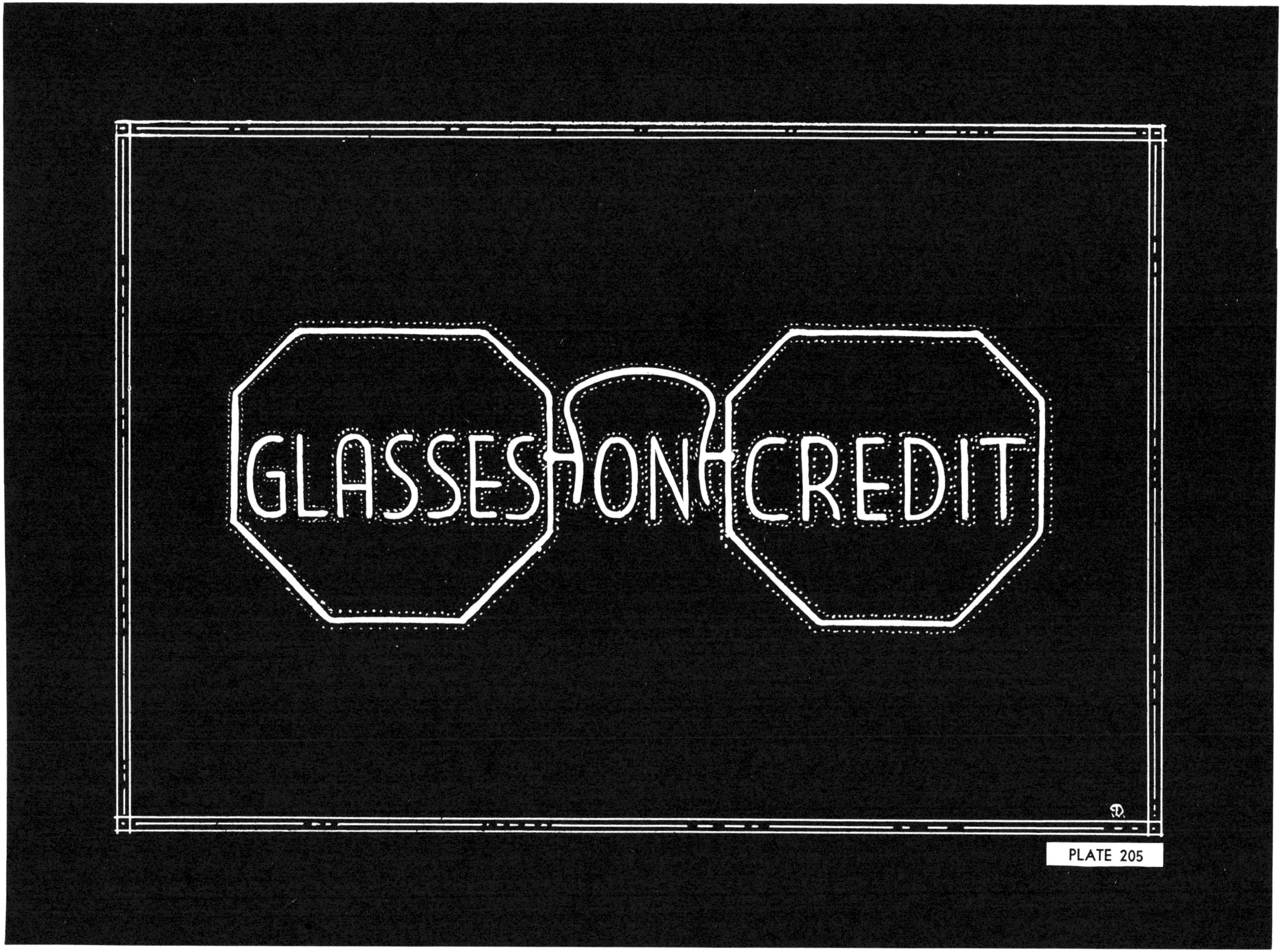

PLATE 205

INDEX TO PLATES

DESIGNS AND SUGGESTIONS WHICH CAN BE READILY ADAPTED FOR USE ON THEATRES — HOTELS — FOOD MARKETS — DEPARTMENT STORES — FURNITURE STORES — etc.

INDEX TO PLATES

INDEX TO PLATES